Sensational
Sugar Animals

Dedication

To my husband Mike, and to the McNaughtons and
Lewises who have always been so supportive.

Sensational
Sugar Animals

FRANCES MCNAUGHTON

Search Press

First published in Great Britain 2012

Search Press Limited
Wellwood, North Farm Road,
Tunbridge Wells, Kent TN2 3DR

Illustrations and text copyright © Frances McNaughton 2012

Photographs by Roddy Paine Photographic Studios

Photographs and design copyright © Search Press Ltd. 2012

ISBN: 978-1-84448-744-8

The Publishers and author can accept no responsibility for any consequences arising from the information, advice or instructions given in this publication.

Suppliers
If you have difficulty in obtaining any of the materials and equipment mentioned in this book, then please visit the Search Press website for details of suppliers:
www.searchpress.com

You are invited to visit the author's website:
www.franklysweet.co.uk

Acknowledgements

Special thanks to Sophie Kersey, Marrianne Mercer and Roddy Paine.

I would also like to thank Pauline Tye for introducing me to sculpting with marzipan many years ago.

Thanks to Marion Frost of Patchwork Cutters for the Mexican paste recipe.

Thanks also to Eddie Spence MBE for his royal icing recipe.

Printed in Malaysia

Contents

Introduction 6

Materials 8

Techniques 12

Sheep 22

Cow 28

Gorilla 34

Beaver 40

Meerkat 46

Fox 52

Lion 58

Pig 64

Brown Bear 70

Kangaroo and Joey 76

Rabbit 82

Rhinoceros 88

Baby Elephant 94

Tortoise 100

Polar Bear 106

Three Cats 112

Bat 120

Index 128

Introduction

I started making cakes and sweets when I was only six years old and loved working my way through my Mum's old cookery book, which was very thick and had lots of old black and white photographs. Three sisters and a brother were available as willing guinea pigs to try out my creations. It also gave me lots of practice over the years as there were plenty of birthdays to make cakes for – early on as an assistant to Mum, and later by myself. I worked in an office after leaving school but carried on making cakes for friends and family. In 1987 I took the plunge and started a cake decorating business from home.

I have always enjoyed many aspects of cake decorating and sugarcraft, including modelling in sugar, making realistic flowers and creating fairies. Teaching sugarcraft has given me a lot of pleasure, and I enjoy passing this on to other people in my teaching and demonstrating. I try to find simple ways of making items in sugar, and in recent years have been able to pass this on to an even larger audience through my books. I wrote *Twenty to Make: Sugar Animals* which appeals to experienced sugarcrafters, beginners and children alike. It is an introduction to sugar modelling, enabling people to make simple animals in a relatively short time with very few items of equipment.

Following on from that book I have created these *Sensational Sugar Animals* for people who would like to make their animals more natural-looking, with realistic colouring. I have kept the models as simple as possible. Experienced sculptors will be able to expand on the animals I have shown, giving each animal even more detail if they wish.

I use a variety of different edible materials for creating the animals, to give slightly different effects. People who enjoy modelling will realise that although I work with edible materials, the shapes can be used to make animals with non-edible modelling clay – various types of air-drying and oven-drying clays are available from craft shops. Sizes can also be scaled down or up to suit your project.

I love the countryside, and together with my husband, Mike, we spend a lot of time walking. We currently live in a small cottage in the country with lots of woodland all round us. Inspired by the animals around me, I could include some of my favourites and I really had fun developing my ideas. The method of laying the 'skin' over some of the animal frames developed from the shape of a sheepskin to form my Sheep, and worked so well that I used it for some of the other animals.

Bats live in the roof of our cottage and can be seen at dusk as they leave to hunt for insects, and at dawn as they return. In the woods behind the house we have a family of truly wild foxes, who never come near the house, but we have been lucky to see the fox cubs at their den in the spring. Our nearest neighbours, who live further down our lane into the woods, had three pigs this year, and six sheep. My own three cats also had to be included, as they are with me when I write the words for each book – usually 'helping' by walking over the keyboard for me!

I hope you will have as much fun making your own animals as I did in making this book, but the real joy is in developing your own variations. Have fun!

Materials

Modelling materials

Mexican paste

This is a sugar modelling paste made with gum tragacanth to make it stronger and to allow it to be rolled out thinly. I have used it to make the bodies of animals which need to be dried hard before covering with skin or fur. It is available commercially or can be made using the following recipe:

Place 227g (8oz) icing sugar (confectioner's sugar) into a bowl.
Add 3 x 5ml teaspoons of gum tragacanth.
Mix the dry ingredients together.
Add 6 x 5ml teaspoons of cold water.
Stir by hand until it becomes crumbly but damp enough to bind together. Add a little more water if it is too dry, or icing sugar if it is too wet. Turn out on to a worktop and knead until pliable.

Place into a plastic bag and leave at room temperature for 12 hours until firm.
Break off a small piece and knead between your palms. Continue kneading between your fingers. Repeat until all the paste is softened. It can be used straight away.
   If you have leftover Mexican paste, wrap each piece in plastic food wrap, place all the pieces into a plastic bag and put it in the freezer. Defrost only the quantity required for each project. Smaller pieces will defrost more quickly. Store paste in an airtight container at room temperature, never in the fridge.

Sugarpaste

Commercially available sugarpaste (known as fondant Icing/rolled fondant in some countries) works best for covering hardened animal bodies. It can be blended and textured, as it stays soft for longer than Mexican or modelling paste. It is the easiest paste to use for making short fur and fluff. I like to use white and champagne colours for the models.

Modelling paste

This can be made by kneading one teaspoon (5ml) of CMC (cellulose gum) to approximately 500g (1lb 2oz) of commercial sugarpaste. It can also be used for making the edible sugar candy sticks and the bodies to be dried in advance.

Flower paste

A simple flower paste can be made by mixing equal amounts of Mexican paste to sugarpaste.

Marzipan

I find that commercially available marzipan works better than most home-made marzipan recipes for sculpting and modelling. Buy the natural, not the coloured type.

Royal icing

This can be made from the following recipe:

90g (3oz) free-range egg white (equivalent to 3 medium eggs)
455g (1lb) of icing sugar
5–7 drops of lemon juice

Ensure that all equipment and bowls are grease-free before you start.
Place the egg whites in the mixing bowl. Stir in the sifted icing sugar slowly. Beat for between 10 and 20 minutes. Mix in the lemon juice.

Royal icing can also be made with dried albumen, or fortified albumen. Follow the instructions on the pack to reconstitute the egg white to 90g (3oz) and follow instructions as for fresh eggs. Royal Icing mix is also available, and is useful for making small amounts. Follow the instructions on the pack.

Edible sugar candy sticks

These can be bought from sweet shops/candy stores, but can also be made in advance (see page 21).

Piping gel

This is commercially available from sugarcraft shops. I used it for extra shine on the Gorilla and Beaver. I also piped it into the eyes to make them look bigger and shinier.

Dark chocolate strands

These can be used as tiny eyes for some of the animals.

Clockwise from top left: Mexican paste, royal icing, sugarpaste, edible sugar candy sticks, dark chocolate strands, piping gel and marzipan.

Tools

The following tools are useful (but not all essential) when sculpting and modelling with sugar.

Turntable This helps by raising the height of the materials you are working on, and means you can turn the project while working on it.

Scourers Experiment with different clean, unused pan scourers to press on to soft paste for various textured effects.

Small non-stick rolling pin For rolling out small pieces of paste.

Palette knife For mixing small amounts of royal icing and for helping to lift paste from your work surface.

Fine palette knife For lifting paste from the work surface; particularly useful for small and fine pieces.

Brushpen Filled with water, this is very useful for dampening the surface of the sugar for sticking pieces together.

Cutting wheel Cuts rolled-out paste easily without dragging. Also for marking lines on the surface of the paste.

Ball tool/dogbone tool For marking rounded indentations.

Textured petal veining tool This can be used for fur effects. The wider end has a semicircle shape for embossing.

Dresden tool Very useful for sculpting, smoothing, shaping, making lines and eye sockets.

Cocktail stick For fine modelling and as a temporary support through some of the models while you are working on them.

Cotton bud For painting confectioner's varnish, and also useful for cleaning up small areas when colouring.

Fine pointed scissors For snipping paste to form long bits of fur, and for removing excess paste.

Various cutters Circles, oval and heart cutters are used in the projects.
Fine mesh tea strainer or sieve This is used for making short pieces of fur or fluff.
Plain piping tubes in various sizes These can be used for texturing, and as tiny round cutters or embossers.
Wet wipes Useful when working in sugar to keep your hands clean. Remember to make sure your hands are dry before handling the paste afterwards.
Jewellery scales For accurate weighing. Inexpensive ones are available online.

Colouring equipment

Edible powder food colours These can be brushed on as a dry powder or painted on mixed with pure food-grade alcohol.

Pure food-grade alcohol (isopropyl alcohol) I prefer using this for painting on to sugar as there is no water which could make the sugar sticky. If it is difficult to obtain, you could use alcohol-based lemon essence, gin or vodka (be careful as these contain water).

Confectioner's varnish For making shiny glazed black eyes in advance (see page 20).

Brushpen This can be filled with alcohol and used for painting on the powder colours.

Confectioner's dusting brush A straight-sided brush which holds powder colour well and is good for dusting exactly where the colour is wanted.

Various soft paintbrushes For painting and for texturing soft royal icing. The finest should be size 0000.

Other materials

Tracing paper For tracing the patterns in the book to make templates.

Kitchen paper For mixing small amounts of powder colour and for working the colour into the confectioner's dusting brush.

Vegetable oil Use sparingly on your work surface, tools and hands to stop the paste from sticking to them.

Icing sugar Used when working with marzipan to stop it from sticking.

Florist's tape and fine florist's wire Used for making the bat's wings (see page 124).

Piping bag Used with the royal icing on the Gorilla, and for applying the piping gel in the eyes.

Techniques

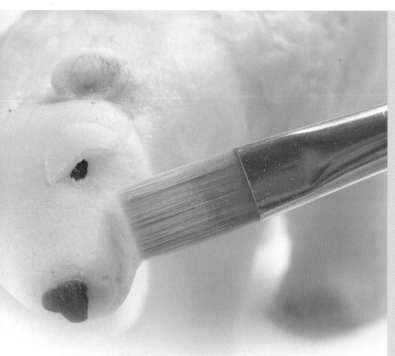

When handling sugarpaste and Mexican paste, use a small amount of vegetable oil on your hands to prevent the paste from sticking. When handling marzipan, it is best to use icing sugar to stop it sticking. Use icing sugar sparingly as it can cause the marzipan to dry and crack.

When sticking any parts together, brush water sparingly to make the surface tacky, not wet. The sugar should then be sticky enough to attach. If water does not stick the pieces together, or if you have breakages, use a small amount of whichever paste you are trying to stick, mix with a small amount of water using a palette knife until it is stringy, and use it as a glue-like filler between the pieces. This is also known as 'gunge'!

Basic shapes

The basic shapes needed to make the animals are shown opposite. They are:

Top row:

A ball

An egg shape/cone

A flat-bottomed cone, made by pinching around the fat end of the egg shape

Second row:

An oval

A pear shape, useful for some animal heads, made by rolling one end of an oval between your fingers

A long ridged cone, used for some of the bodies, made by pinching gently along the length of the long cone

Third row:

An arm or leg used for the Gorilla, made with a sausage shape and rolled in the middle between two fingers

A head with pointed ears used for the Three Cats, made with a ball shape, pinched to form two pointed ears

Fourth row:

A ball-ended long cone used for some of the legs

A drumstick used for some animals where the head and body are in line, made by rolling one end of a sausage shape between two fingers

Adding texture

Fur effects and textured skin can be made in a number of ways; experiment with different kitchen items and tools to achieve different effects.

Scourers

Ordinary household scourers can be used to add texture to your sugar animals to suggest fur or other features. Buy scourers with finer and looser mesh so that you can achieve different textures.

Tools

Use the thin end of the Dresden tool to create fur.

The wider end of the Dresden tool can be used to create a looser, bolder texture.

A palette knife can also be used to create the effect of fine fur.

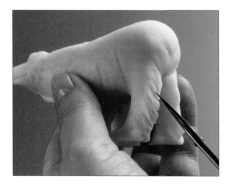

Fine pointed scissors can be used to snip into your sugar animals to create the texture of long fur, as in the Polar Bear project shown here.

Making fur with a sieve or tea strainer

Push sugarpaste or marzipan through the mesh of a sieve or tea strainer to make short fur or fluff. Experiment with different sizes of mesh for thin or thicker strands.

1 Push sugarpaste through a fine mesh sieve or tea strainer.

2 The sugarpaste 'fur' that emerges from the mesh is delicate. Pick it up carefully with a palette knife.

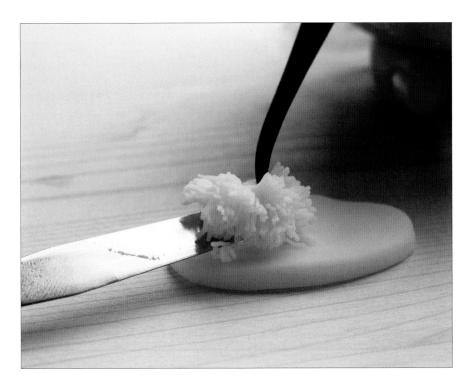

3 Dampen the animal's surface before attaching the sugarpaste fur to it. Place it carefully with the aid of a tool if necessary.

Making a piping bag

A piping bag can be made simply as shown below, or you can use a ready-made one, available from sugarcraft and cook shops.

1 Cut an equilateral triangle of greaseproof or parchment paper.

2 Roll it into a cone shape as shown.

3 Complete the cone and fold over the points to secure it.

Texturing with royal icing

Royal icing can be used to create a textured fur effect, which is useful for any animal where you want a more defined fur coat. The steps below show how to make the fur for the Gorilla (see page 34). The final Gorilla is black and grey, but I only added enough colour to the royal icing to make it grey. Adding a lot of colour can affect the way the royal icing dries. The final black colour is dusted on to the dry royal icing.

1 Pour a little black edible powder food colour into royal icing.

3 Put the grey royal icing into a piping bag and pipe it on to the Gorilla in random squiggles.

2 Mix the powder in to produce a grey paste.

4 Wet a no. 2 brush with water, dry it a little with kitchen paper and use it to drag the edges of the grey royal icing, creating the texture of fur. Allow this part to dry while you work on another part of the Gorilla.

5 Add more squiggles of royal icing over the edges of the dried part.

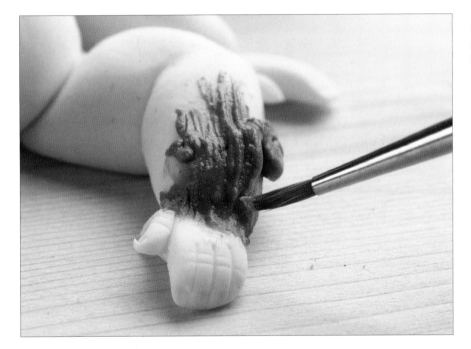

6 Once again, drag the edges of the squiggled royal icing both upwards and downwards to create fur.

The grey royal icing begins to look like fur. The finished Gorilla project is on page 39.

Colouring techniques

I made the animals without adding any colour to the original paste. This is because adding colour can change the consistency of the paste, and I prefer to work with the same consistency throughout. To make the animals look more realistic, I colour the final model with edible powders and edible paint.

Dusting

Different colours and shades of edible powder food colour can be blended on kitchen paper with a confectioner's dusting brush or paper tissue to achieve the effect you want on your animal.

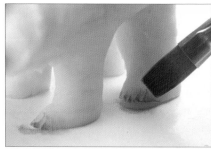 

1 Place dark brown edible powder food colour on kitchen paper and pick it up with a confectioner's dusting brush.

2 Dust the Polar Bear's toes. The sugarpaste is slightly damp and takes up the colour from the powder.

3 Dust the ears. The colour helps to add form to the bear.

4 Dust the Polar Bear's face with white edible powder food colour to add highlights.

5 Finish adding detail to the Polar Bear with the dark brown powder. It helps to bring out details like the mouth.

Painting

To obtain different effects, some animals can be dusted with edible powder food colour first, and then the detail is painted in as shown below.

This cat had already been dusted before painting. Mix pure food-grade alcohol with dark brown edible powder food colour and use a no. 2 paintbrush to paint on the cat's markings. Use the brush slightly dryer where you want to add texture.

Painting fur

Mix pure food-grade alcohol with brown edible powder food colour and drop it into the dried fur using a paintbrush or brushpen. Make sure the mixture is very wet so that it coats the fur easily, but do not use any water as this will dissolve the sugar.

Glazed black eyes

Make these eyes in advance and store them in an airtight container when they are totally dry; they will then keep for months and be available for any modelling project. A very small amount of paste, as shown below, will make many eyes. The glaze helps to keep the black powder stuck to the paste so that your fingers stay clean when handling the eyes. It will also make the eyes shiny, even if you do not finish them with piping gel.

1 Roll out Mexican paste thinly. Mix pure food-grade alcohol with black edible powder food colour and use a brushpen or brush to paint the Mexican paste. Allow to dry.

2 Use a cotton bud to apply confectioner's varnish over the paint. Allow to dry, and paint on a second coat. Allow to dry overnight.

3 Use a no. 2 piping nozzle to cut out tiny eyes.

4 You will need to use a tool to push the eye out of the nozzle. Once the eyes are totally dry and hard, they can be stored for a few months so that they are always ready to use.

Piping gel eyes

To make the eyes look shinier and larger, put a little piping gel into a piping bag. Snip a tiny amount off the tip of the piping bag and pipe a little gel into the eye.

The Polar Bear's eye shown before and after piping gel was added, showing the shine and magnification it creates.

Cats' eyes

Cats' eyes can be made in different colours. They could be made in advance so that they are dry, or they could be used straight away.

1 Make a tiny ball of green sugarpaste and cut it in half.

2 Dampen the eye sockets with water.

3 Push the green eyes into the sockets using a Dresden tool.

4 Mix black edible powder food colour with pure food-grade alcohol and use a size 0000 brush to paint the cat's distinctive irises. Allow to dry.

5 Use a piping bag to pipe clear piping gel into the eyes.

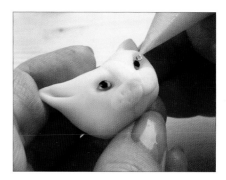

Making edible sugar candy sticks

If the candy sticks used in the projects are unavailable, it is easy to make your own. Use Mexican paste, modelling paste or sugarpaste with a pinch of CMC (cellulose gum) added to strengthen it.

1 Roll out the paste into a long cylinder shape.

2 Use a palette knife to cut the cylinder into lengths as shown, then leave them to dry until hard – it could take a few days.

Sheep

This was the animal that gave me the idea of making the body first and the sheepskin afterwards. One of the advantages of this is that you can play around with the colours of the coat and the head and make different breeds of sheep.

The pattern for the sheepskin.

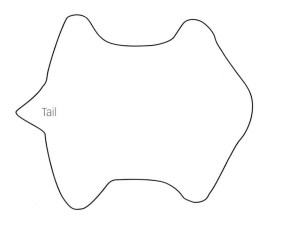

Tail

You will need

5g (¹/₆oz) of Mexican paste

Edible sugar candy sticks

105g (3²/₃oz) of white/champagne sugarpaste

Rolling pin

Cutting wheel

Scourer

Fine pointed scissors

Dark chocolate strands

Palette knife

Dresden tool

Edible powder food colours: soft natural pink and dark brown

Confectioner's dusting brush

Kitchen paper

No. 2 paintbrush

Pure food-grade alcohol

Piping gel in a piping bag

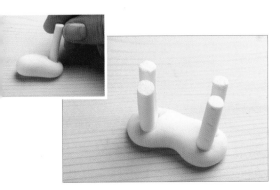

1 To make the base for the sheep, make an oval from 5g (¹/₆oz) of Mexican paste. It should be 3cm (1¹/₈in) long. Push in four 3cm (1¹/₈in) lengths of candy stick for legs as shown.

2 Stand up the sheep base and leave it to dry, preferably overnight.

3 Roll out 100g (3½oz) of sugarpaste to 3mm (¹/₈in) thick.

4 Photocopy or trace the pattern shown above and cut it out to make a template. Place the template on the rolled out sugarpaste and use the cutting wheel to cut out the shape for the sheepskin.

5 Press the cut-out sheepskin with a scourer to create the texture of wool.

6 Dampen the underside of the sheepskin and stick it to the sheep base.

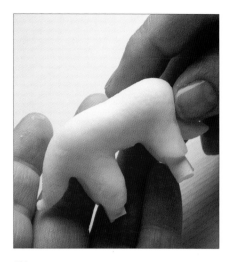

7 Press the sheepskin into the body, shaping it around the legs.

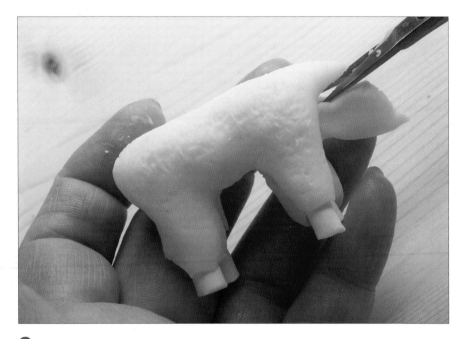

8 Pinch the sheepskin to seal it under the tail, then cut the tail to shape with fine pointed scissors.

9 Press an indentation with your finger for the neck.

10 Take a 2g (¹/₁₂oz) ball of sugarpaste and roll one end to narrow it to a 2cm (¾in) cone for the head.

11 Push in a chocolate strand for each eye.

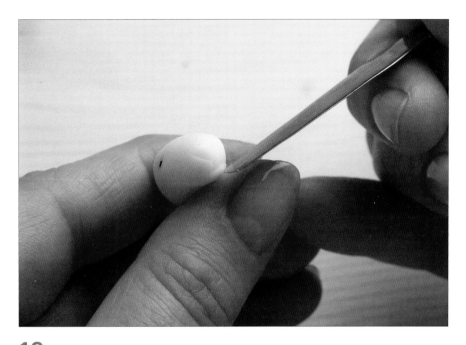

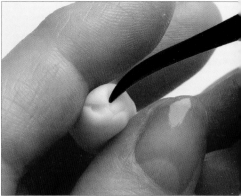

13 Place a finger over the top of the nose and push up the nostrils using the Dresden tool.

12 Mark a 'Y' shape for the nose and a line across for the mouth using the palette knife.

14 Dampen the indentation with water for the neck. Press the head on to the body.

15 For each ear, take a tiny piece of sugarpaste and make a 1cm (³/₈in) long pointed cone, then press it with the Dresden tool to create a hollow. Repeat to make a second ear

16 Pinch one end of each ear to shape them.

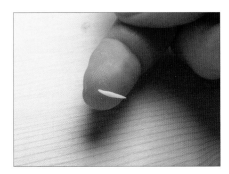

17 Make a tiny roll of sugarpaste 1cm (³/₈in) long.

18 Cut the roll in half with the palette knife to make the sheep's eyelids.

19 Dampen the area above the eyes and stick the eyelids on. Move them about to place them more precisely with the Dresden tool.

20 Dampen and attach the ears as shown.

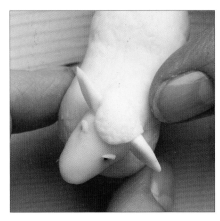

21 Shape a 2cm (¾in) oval of sugarpaste to make a tuft of wool, and texture it with the scourer.

22 Dampen the tuft of wool and stick it on to the head.

23 Blend the tuft of wool in with your fingers.

The modelled Sheep, ready for colouring.

Left and opposite

The finished Sheep. To add colour, use a soft pink edible powder food colour with a confectioner's dusting brush to gently brush the nose, mouth and inside the ears. Brush the feet and under the nose with dark brown edible powder food colour.

Cow

The cow is made in a similar way to the sheep, and therefore alternatives to this Friesian breed can easily be made using different colours for the cowhide and head.

The pattern for the cowhide.

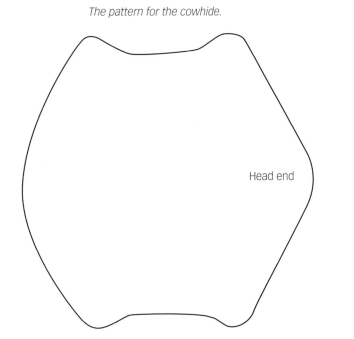

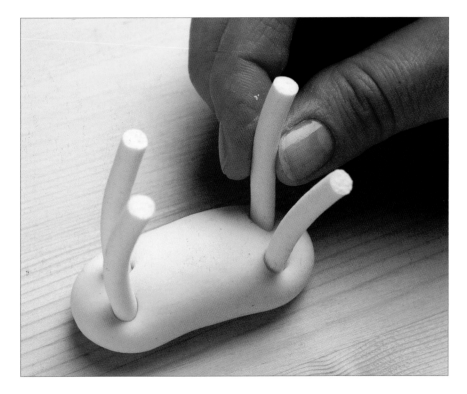

You will need

30g (1oz) of Mexican or modelling paste

Edible sugar candy sticks

Rolling pin

106g (3¾oz) of white/champagne sugarpaste

30g (1oz) of black sugarpaste

Cutting wheel

Fine pointed scissors

Dresden tool

Fine mesh sieve or tea strainer

Palette knife

Two glazed black eyes (see page 20)

Edible powder food colours: soft natural pink, dark brown and black

Confectioner's dusting brush

Kitchen paper

Pure food-grade alcohol

No. 2 paintbrush

Piping gel in a piping bag

1 Roll 25g (just under 1oz) of Mexican or modelling paste into a 6cm (2⅜in) sausage and press in four 4.5cm (1¾in) lengths of candy stick for legs as shown.

2 Stand the body up on the legs and press in a 2.5cm (1in) length of candy stick for the neck. Leave the body to dry, preferably overnight.

3 Photocopy or trace the pattern for the cowhide and cut it out to make a template. Roll out 100g (3½in) of sugarpaste to 3mm (⅛in) thick and cut round the template with a cutting wheel. Form blobs from 30g (1oz) of black sugarpaste into random blobs and flatten them. Push them into the cowhide to look like the coat of a Friesian cow. If the black sugarpaste does not stick, dampen it slightly with water.

4 Dampen the underside of the cowhide, place it on the cow and shape it round the legs.

5 Shape the cowhide round the cow's neck.

6 Trim the cow's neck to size with fine pointed scissors.

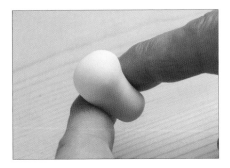

7 Make the head from a 5g (¹/₆oz) ball of sugarpaste. Roll it to 3cm (1¹/₈in) long and make one end narrower.

8 Press in eye sockets with the Dresden tool.

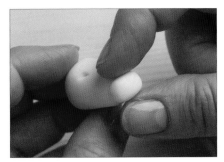

9 Make a pea-sized ball of sugarpaste and attach it to the face to make a muzzle.

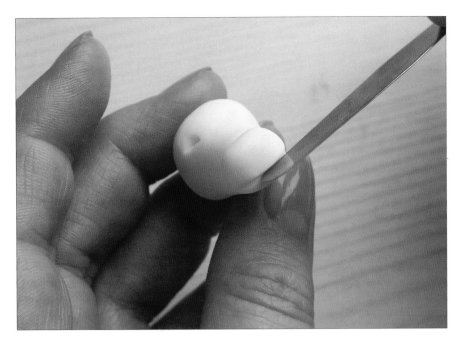

10 Mark the mouth with a palette knife as shown.

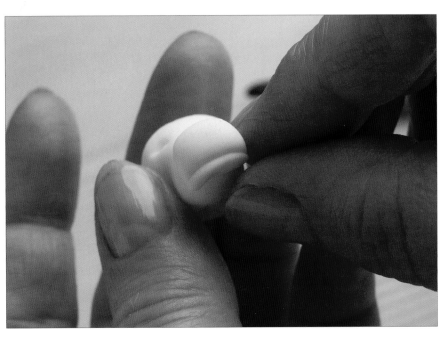

11 Pinch the edges of the mouth to turn it down.

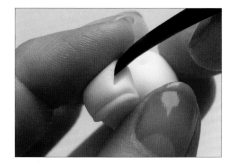

12 Place your finger over the muzzle and use the Dresden tool to push up nostrils as shown.

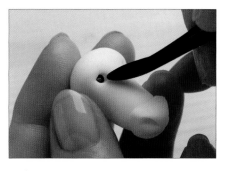

13 Take two glazed black eyes (see page 20) and push them into the sockets using the Dresden tool.

14 Make two tiny sausage shapes from sugarpaste and place them over the eyes as brows. Blend them in with your finger.

15 Push the head on the body as shown.

16 Make ears as for the Sheep (page 24, steps 15 and 16), but slightly larger. Dampen them and stick them in place.

17 Push sugarpaste through a tea strainer to create a tuft of hair and take it off with the palette knife. Dampen the top of the head between the ears.

18 Place the hair on the cow's head.

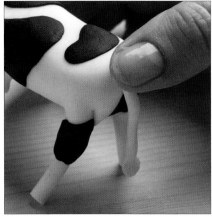

19 Roll a 4cm (1½in) long tail shape from 5g (¹⁄₆oz) of Mexican or modelling paste and mark the ends with the cutting wheel.

20 Dampen and attach the tail.

The modelled Cow, ready for colouring.

Above and opposite

The finished Cow. Use a soft pink edible powder food colour with a confectioner's dusting brush to gently colour the nose, mouth and inside the ears. Brush the feet, inside the nostrils and the mouth with dark brown powder food colour, then brush around the eyes with black powder food colour. Mix black powder food colour with a few drops of pure food-grade alcohol to a painting consistency. Paint the tips of the ears and the sides of the face using a no. 2 paintbrush. Finish by adding piping gel to the eyes.

Gorilla

This ape certainly has attitude! To help when making his face, look up pictures of real gorillas on the internet – you will be surprised at how much easier it is to get right when you have the real thing to copy.

You will need

144g (5oz) of Mexican paste or modelling paste

6g (¼oz) of white/champagne sugarpaste

Edible sugar candy stick

Dresden tool

Fine pointed scissors

Palette knife

2cm (¾in) heart cutter

Grey royal icing (see page 16)

Black edible powder food colour

Pure food-grade alcohol

No. 2 paintbrush

Confectioner's dusting brush

Kitchen paper

Piping gel in a piping bag

Two glazed black eyes (see page 20)

1 Make an oval from 60g (2oz) of Mexican or modelling paste for the body. Insert a candy stick down through the whole body to the work surface. Use a Dresden tool to mark the chest and tummy button.

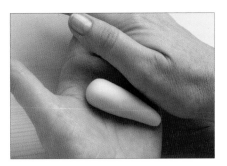

2 Make four cone shapes, each from 15g (½oz) of Mexican paste, for the gorilla's limbs.

3 Use two fingers to roll the middle of each limb to create joints.

4 Bend the arms and legs.

5 Make four ovals, each from 1g (1/24oz) of Mexican paste, and flatten them to make hands and feet.

6 Use fine pointed scissors to cut a triangle out of each to form a thumb.

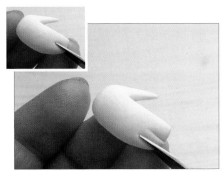

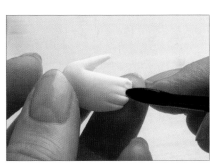

7 Flatten the ends of the fingers (and toes) slightly on all four.

8 Snip into the hand half-way across with the scissors, to divide the hand in half. Then snip half-way across each half to form the fingers. Repeat for the other hand and feet.

9 Mark finger and toenails with the end of the Dresden tool.

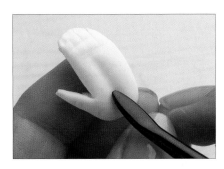

10 Use the palette knife to make markings on the palms.

11 Use the Dresden tool to mark tendons on the back of the hand.

12 Press the inside of the hands to give them a cupped shape.

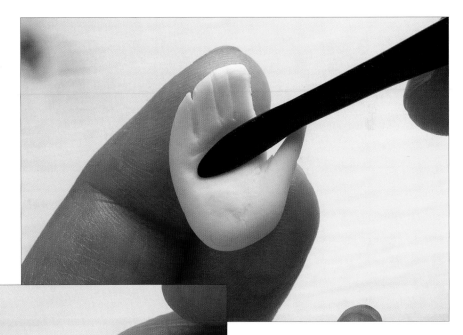

A finished hand/foot. You should end up with two left and two right hands/feet.

13 Before attaching a leg, press on the part to be attached with your finger to flatten it a little.

14 Brush the pressed area with water and attach the legs, using the finished Gorilla picture as a guide. Attach the feet.

15 Attach the arms and hands in the same way, following the finished Gorilla picture.

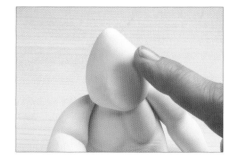

16 Make the head from 20g (²/₃oz) of Mexican or modelling paste, shaped into a fat cone 3.5cm (1³/₈in) high. Flatten the bottom as shown. Use a candy stick to make a hole in the head and place it on the neck.

17 Flatten the face with your finger.

18 Use a 2cm (¾in) heart cutter to cut out a heart from 3g (¹/₈oz) of sugarpaste. Sugarpaste is used for the details as it stays soft and malleable longer than Mexican or modelling paste.

19 Make a 2g (¹/₁₂oz) ball of the same sugarpaste for the muzzle and stick this on to the heart.

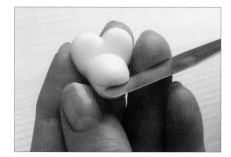

20 Use the palette knife to mark the mouth.

21 Mark a line down the centre of the muzzle with the Dresden tool.

22 Place a finger above the muzzle and use the Dresden tool to push up holes for nostrils.

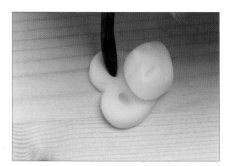

23 Mark the eye sockets with the Dresden tool.

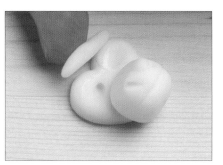

24 Make a 2cm (¾in) sausage from a tiny piece of sugarpaste for the brow and attach this to the face.

25 Mark the brow with the Dresden tool to create wrinkles.

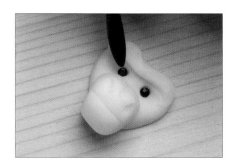

26 Take two previously made glazed black eyes (see page 20) and press these into the eye sockets.

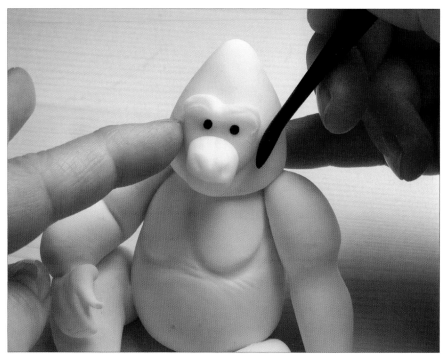

27 Dampen the back of the face and stick it gently on to the front of the head. Blend it in using the Dresden tool.

28 Roll tiny balls of sugarpaste for the ears, and stick them on as shown. Use a Dresden tool to hollow them out.

The modelled Gorilla, ready for colouring.

Left and opposite

The coloured Gorilla. To make the fur, pipe grey royal icing as shown on page 16 and brush with a damp no. 2 paintbrush to make a fur texture. Keep the brush clean and damp, drying slightly on kitchen paper each time it is cleaned of any drying royal icing. Work on a small area at a time, allowing each area to dry before piping the next piece of royal icing on to a different part of the Gorilla. Gradually cover the legs, arms, back and head with the fur effect. Allow the Gorilla to dry, then place him on a piece of kitchen paper, as the next bit of colouring can be messy! Use a confectioner's dusting brush to dust the royal icing with black edible powder food colour. The top of the head and the back can be left grey is you want him to be a silverback gorilla. Mix black powder food colour with a few drops of pure food-grade alcohol to a painting consistency. Paint the tips of the ears, the face, tummy, hands and feet. When the black painting is dry, paint the same areas with piping gel to make him look leathery. Finish by adding piping gel to the eyes.

Beaver

I fell in love with beavers after reading *The Lion, the Witch and the Wardrobe* by C.S. Lewis. I also find their lifestyle quite amazing – they cut down trees with their incredibly strong teeth and shift the trees and branches to form dams and build their lodges. Beavers have unusual flat tails to help with swimming and these are quite a feature when making the model.

You will need

Tiny amount of golden brown Mexican paste

Palette knife

106g (3¾oz) white/ champagne sugarpaste

Tiny amount of black sugarpaste

Ball tool

Dresden tool

Edible powder food colour: dark brown and black

Confectioner's dusting brush

Kitchen paper

Piping gel in a piping bag

No. 2 paintbrush

Two glazed black eyes (see page 20)

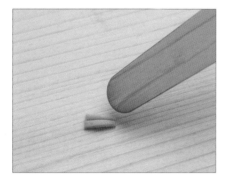

1 Make a 4mm (³/₁₆in) rectangle from golden brown Mexican paste. Mark it down the middle with a palette knife to make the beaver's front teeth, and leave to dry, preferably overnight.

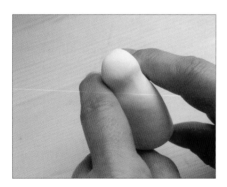

2 Roll 30g (1oz) of champagne or white sugarpaste to a 6cm (2³/₈in) sausage and roll it between your fingers to shape the neck.

3 Bend the head forwards a little to create a realistic posture.

4 Make two tiny balls of sugarpaste and stick them on the face to make the muzzle.

5 Place a finger behind the head and push the rounded end of the ball tool into the head to shape an ear. Repeat for the second ear.

6 Make eye sockets with the sharper end of the Dresden tool.

7 Push in two glazed black eyes (see page 20).

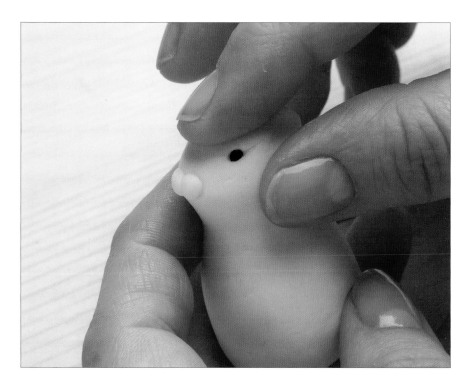

8 Squeeze the eye sockets together a little around the eyes.

9 Make tiny sausage shapes from sugarpaste for brows. Place them and blend them in a little with the Dresden tool.

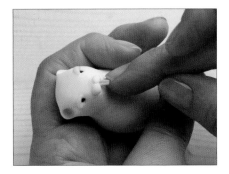

10 Push the teeth in under the muzzle.

11 Take a tiny ball of black sugarpaste and squeeze it into a triangle for the nose.

12 Dampen and attach the nose, then use the Dresden tool to push up two nostrils.

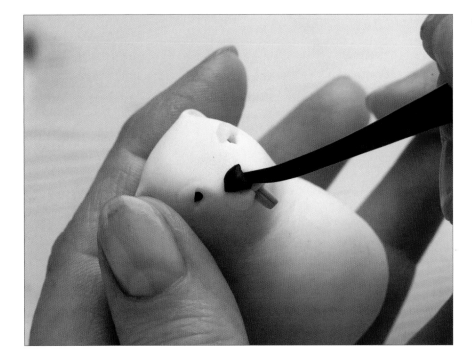

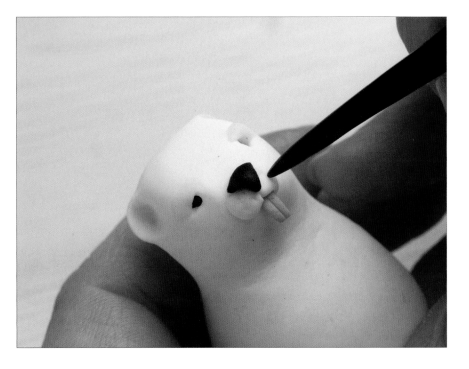

13 Use the Dresden tool to mark dots for whiskers.

14 Make each back foot with 0.5g (¹/₄₈oz) of sugarpaste shaped into a 1.5cm (⁵/₈in) cone. Press the narrow end with the Dresden tool four times to create webbing.

15 Dampen the feet and attach them under the body as shown.

16 Make a 4cm (1½in) long sausage shape with 3g (¹/₈oz) of sugarpaste. Flatten it, and make marks across it with the palette knife. Make marks across the first marks to complete the Beaver's tail.

17 Dampen the tail and attach it to the Beaver.

18 To make each front leg, roll 0.5g (¹/₄₈oz) of sugarpaste into a 2cm (¾in) sausage and bend it to make a joint.

19 Make three marks with the palette knife to create the paws.

The modelled Beaver, ready for colouring.

20 Dampen the front legs and push them both on at the same time.

21 When the sugarpaste is dry, scratch it with the palette knife to create the texture of fur.

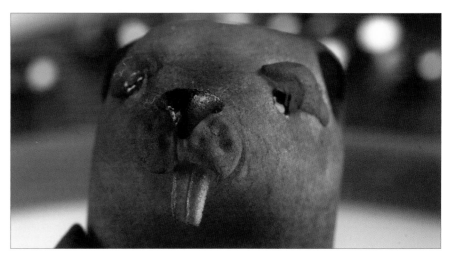

Left, above and opposite

The finished Beaver. Brush all over with dark brown edible powder food colour, using a confectioner's dusting brush. Brush the toes, the tips of the ears and the brows gently with a little black powder food colour on a no. 2 paintbrush. With piping gel, paint over the tail, nose and teeth. Finish by adding piping gel to the eyes.

Meerkat

Meerkats have very appealing faces with lovely shiny eyes. In life they form large family groups who all look after each other, and take turns looking out for danger so that they can warn the whole group. They have become very popular in recent years making them a good subject for cake decoration.

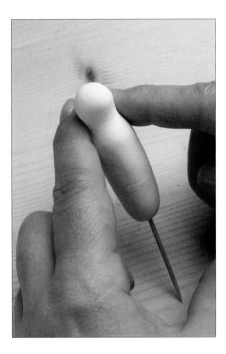

1 Shape 15g (½oz) of Mexican or modelling paste into a sausage shape, and stick a cocktail stick through it lengthwise for ease of handling. Shape the neck by rolling it between two fingers.

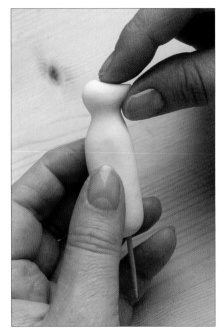

2 Pinch the head out to a point to form the nose.

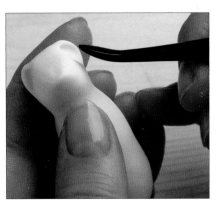

3 Hollow out the ears with the wide end of the Dresden tool.

You will need

20g (²/₃oz) of Mexican or modelling paste

A small amount of white/champagne sugarpaste

Cocktail stick

Dresden tool

Palette knife

Edible powder food colours: dark brown and autumn gold

Confectioner's dusting brush

Kitchen paper

Piping gel in a piping bag

No. 2 paintbrush

Two glazed black eyes (see page 20)

4 Make the nostrils with the other end of the Dresden tool.

5 Mark the mouth with a curving stroke of the palette knife.

6 Press the narrow end of the Dresden tool into the face to create eye sockets.

7 Take two glazed black eyes (see page 20) and press them into the eye sockets.

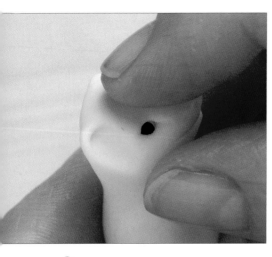

8 Pinch the eye sockets together a little to make more realistic eyes.

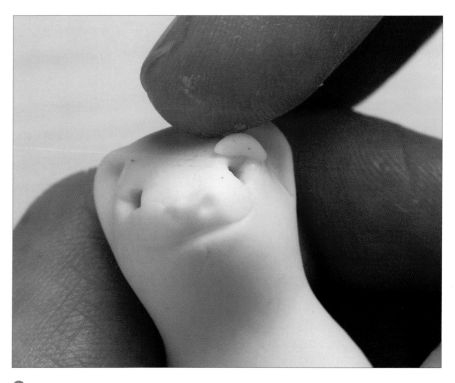

9 Make tiny sausage shapes from sugarpaste for brows. Dampen them and press them on over the eyes. Blend them in with your fingers.

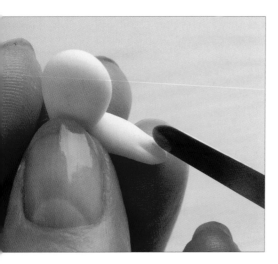

10 To make each back leg, shape 1g (1/24oz) of Mexican or modelling paste into a cone, bend it in the middle to create a knee, and use a palette knife to mark toes.

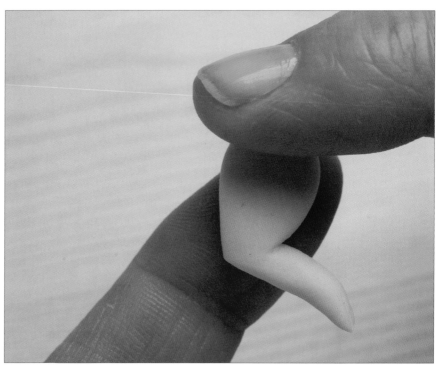

11 Press the legs from the side to flatten them ready for attachment.

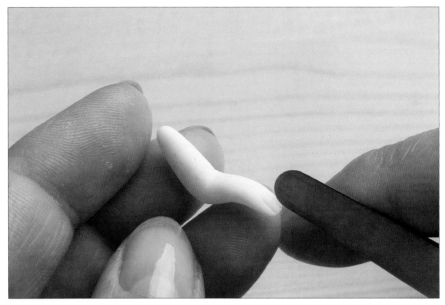

13 For each front leg, shape 0.5g (¹⁄₄₈oz) of Mexican or modelling paste into a 3cm (1¼in) sausage, bend it into a 'Z' shape and mark toes with a palette knife.

12 Push the back legs on to the body as shown.

14 Dampen and attach the front legs as shown.

15 Pull the cocktail stick out from the Meerkat. Make a sausage shape from 0.5g (¹⁄₄₈oz) of Mexican paste and stick it on as shown, for the tail.

The modelled Meerkat, ready for colouring.

Left and opposite

The finished Meerkat. Brush it all over with the confectioner's dusting brush and autumn gold edible powder food colour. Brush the toes, the tip of the tail, tips of the ears, mouth, eyes and the top of the head gently with a little dark brown powder food colour on the no. 2 paintbrush. Finish by adding piping gel to the eyes.

Fox

Foxes in the wild are really beautiful animals. Unfortunately in recent years they have lost favour as they have become more used to living in town and city centres, causing problems by rummaging through rubbish for food. However, they are still very popular with many people and seeing them in your garden is often a real treat.

You will need

24g (just under 1oz) of Mexican paste

Cocktail stick

Palette knife

5g (1/6oz) of white/champagne sugarpaste

Dresden tool

Two glazed black eyes (see page 20)

Tiny amount of black sugarpaste

Fine mesh sieve or tea strainer

Edible powder food colours: dark brown and terracotta/skin tone

Confectioner's dusting brush

Kitchen paper

Pure food-grade alcohol

No. 2 paintbrush

Piping gel in a piping bag

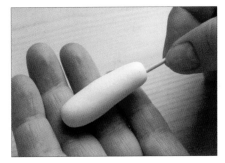

1 Make the body by rolling 7g (1/4oz) of Mexican paste into a sausage shape. Insert a cocktail stick for ease of handling, oiled so that you can remove it easily later.

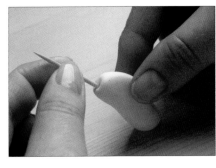

2 Pinch the body to create the curve of the shoulders, then leave it to dry, preferably overnight.

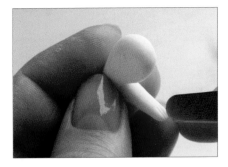

3 To make each back leg, take 1.5g (1/16oz) of Mexican paste and roll it into a 4cm (1½in) carrot shape. Fold this in half at right angles to make the knee and flatten the rounded end. Make marks with the palette knife for toes.

4 Dampen the back legs, attach them to the body and pinch them together.

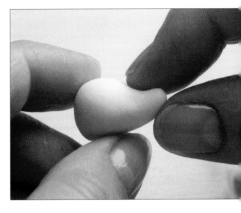

5 Make the head from 3g (1/8oz) of sugarpaste, rolled into a ball. Bring it to a point so that it is 2cm (¾in) long.

6 Using the Dresden tool, make a mark on either side of the nose, going from the nose to the side of the head. This is a guide to where the eyes will go.

7 Make holes with the Dresden tool for eye sockets, then push in two glazed black eyes (see page 20).

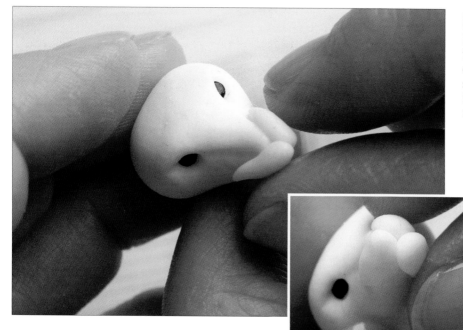

8 Pinch the eye sockets together a little. Roll two tiny sausage shapes from sugarpaste and press them either side of the nose to create the snout. Pinch and blend them in place. Make another tiny ball and press it under the chin.

9 Make two tiny sausages of sugarpaste and press these over the eyes to make brows.

10 Make the ears in the same way as for the sheep on page 24 and attach them to the head.

11 Make a ball of black sugarpaste, squeeze it into a triangle for the nose, and stick it in place. Push up nostrils on either side of the nose with the Dresden tool.

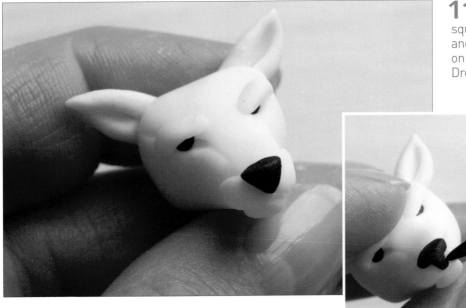

12 Push sugarpaste through a tea strainer to create fur and lift it off with a palette knife. Dampen the fox's tummy and press on the fur.

13 To make each front leg, roll 1g (¹/₂₄oz) of Mexican paste into a carrot shape. Check it against the body to make sure it is the right length. Pinch and curve the pointed end to make a paw.

14 Dampen and attach the front legs as shown.

15 Make a thin tail from sugarpaste, roughly the same length as a front leg.

16 Make a length of fur by pressing sugarpaste through the tea strainer as before. Pick it up on the palette knife and attach it to the dampened tail to make the fox's brush.

17 Attach the brush to the body.

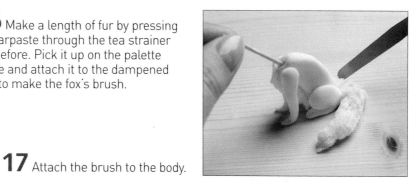

18 Make more fur using the tea strainer and sugarpaste, dampen the fox's cheeks and attach the fur.

The modelled Fox, ready for colouring.

This page and opposite

The finished Fox. Brush terracotta/ skintone edible powder food colour over the body, legs and head using the confectioner's dusting brush, avoiding the fur which will be left white. Gently brush dark brown powder on the feet, inside the ears, over the brows, down towards the nose, and lightly over the mouth, using the no. 2 paintbrush. Mix terracotta/ skin tone powder with pure food-grade alcohol to form a runny paint consistency. Still using the no. 2 paintbrush, drop large drops of the paint on to the body end of the Fox's brush, leaving the tip white. Finish by adding piping gel to the eyes.

Lion

A few years ago I had the pleasure of being able to meet and hold Samira, a lion cub at Port Lympne Wild Animal Park in Kent. She was being hand-reared by one of the keepers as she had sustained a spinal injury at birth. I was struck by how soft her fur was, and by her beautiful eyes. Lions have always been a favourite with children and cake decorators alike.

You will need

90g (3oz) of Mexican or modelling paste

10g (⅓oz) of champagne sugarpaste

Tiny amounts of golden brown and black sugarpaste

Edible sugar candy stick

Palette knife

Dresden tool

Cutting wheel

Ball tool

Fine mesh sieve or tea strainer

Edible powder food colours: autumn gold and dark brown

Confectioner's dusting brush

Kitchen paper

Pure food-grade alcohol

No. 2 paintbrush

Piping gel in a piping bag

Two glazed black eyes (see page 20)

1 Take 45g (1½oz) of Mexican or modelling paste and roll it into a carrot shape for the body.

2 Pinch to create a ridge for the lion's back, and curve the thinner end round a little.

3 Push in a 4cm (1½in) length of candy stick for the neck at the fatter end.

4 Make each leg by rolling 6g (¼oz) of Mexican or modelling paste into a narrow 7cm (2¾in) cone.

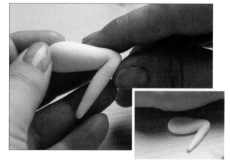

5 Bend the leg in the middle to make the knee joint. Flatten the fat end as shown.

6 Make three marks on the paw with the palette knife to create toes. Make four legs in the same way.

7 Dampen one of the back legs and attach it under the body as shown.

8 Attach the second back leg in the same way, but on top of the body as shown, and at a slightly different angle.

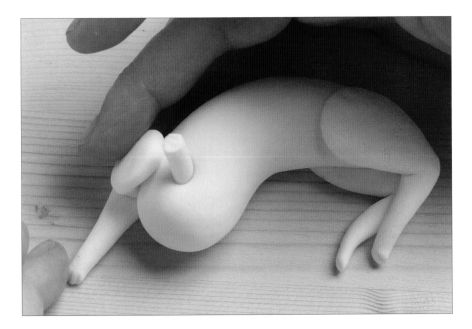

9 Attach the third leg at the front, as shown. The paw should reach out in front with its underside flat on the work surface.

10 Attach the opposite front leg in the same position.

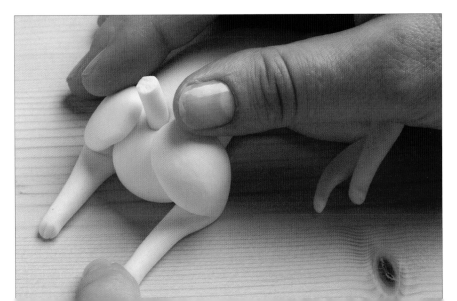

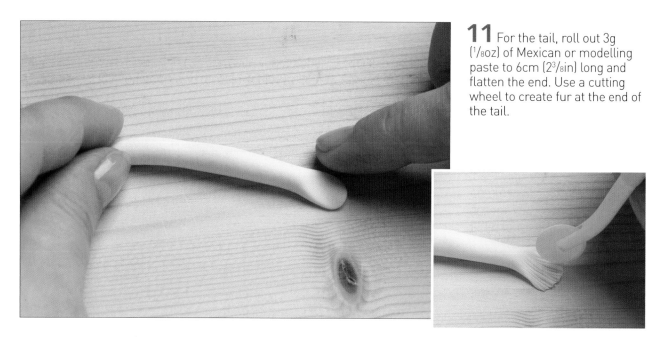

11 For the tail, roll out 3g (¹/₈oz) of Mexican or modelling paste to 6cm (2³/₈in) long and flatten the end. Use a cutting wheel to create fur at the end of the tail.

12 Attach the tail.

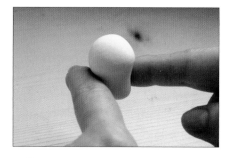

13 Take 14g (just under ½oz) of Mexican or modelling paste for the head and roll it into a pear shape 3cm (1¹/₈in) long.

14 The features are made from ordinary sugarpaste, as it is stays soft and malleable for longer. Make two tiny balls for the cheeks, dampen them and attach them to the narrow end of the face.

15 Make another ball the same size, roll it into a cone and attach it underneath for the chin. Flattening it and blend it in.

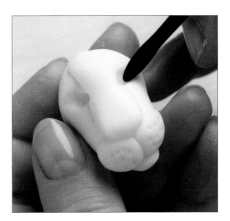

16 Roll a 2cm (¾in) cone for the top of the face from 1g (¹/₂₄oz) of sugarpaste. Dampen the top of the face and attach and blend in the cone.

17 Make dots for whiskers with the Dresden tool.

18 Use the flatter end of the Dresden tool to create eye sockets.

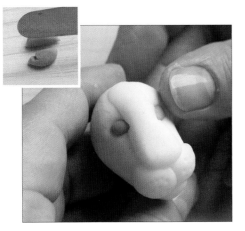

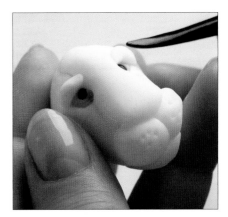

19 Make a tiny ball of golden brown sugarpaste and cut it in half with the palette knife to make two ovals. Push these into the eye sockets.

20 Push in two glazed black eyes (see page 20) for the pupils.

21 Make tiny carrot shapes from champagne sugarpaste for the brows, and dampen and attach these above the eyes.

22 Push a hole in the base of the head using a candy stick, then attach the head to the neck.

23 Take a tiny piece of black sugarpaste, pinch it into a triangle for the nose and attach it. Mark nostrils with the Dresden tool.

24 Push champagne sugarpaste through the tea strainer to make the mane. Dampen the head and attach the mane all around it.

25 Make each ear from a small ball of sugarpaste, and hollow them out with the ball tool.

26 Attach the ears and finish shaping them in place.

The modelled Lion, ready for colouring.

Above and opposite

The finished Lion. Brush gently all over with autumn gold edible powder food colour using a confectioner's dusting brush. Apply slightly more colour over the ears and down the face. Then lightly brush dark brown edible powder colour over the feet, the tip of the tail, inside the ears, the eyebrows, and the mouth. Mix a little autumn gold and dark brown together with pure food-grade alcohol. The mixture needs to be very runny so that the colour runs into the fur on the mane. Finish by adding piping gel to the eyes.

Pig

As a vegetarian, I have only ever looked at pigs as the lovely animals that they are, not the way my husband sees them – as various cuts of meat! Our neighbours recently had three pigs, and we would go and say 'hello' to them on our regular walks. We were always greeted by the three of them, who seemed happy to see us. There are many different breeds of pig which you can make simply by adapting the colours and shapes slightly from my original model.

You will need

56g (just under 2oz) of Mexican paste

25g (just under 1oz) of white/champagne sugarpaste

Two glazed black eyes (see page 20)

Fine pointed scissors

Dresden tool

Edible sugar candy sticks

Fine mesh sieve or tea strainer

Cutting wheel

Palette knife

Edible powder food colours: terracotta/skin tone, white and dark brown

Confectioner's dusting brush

Kitchen paper

Piping gel in a piping bag

1 Make the body from 55g (just under 2oz) of Mexican paste, rolled into an 8cm (3¹⁄₈in) sausage shape.

2 Pinch the end to create the pig's snout.

3 Use fine pointed scissors to snip across the snout to make the mouth.

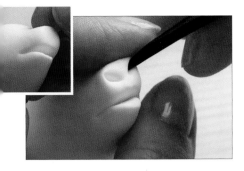

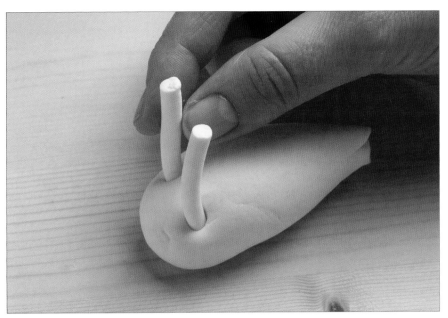

4 Press the snout to flatten it, then make indentations with the Dresden tool for nostrils.

5 Lay the pig body on its back and push in two 4cm (1½in) lengths of candy stick for the back legs.

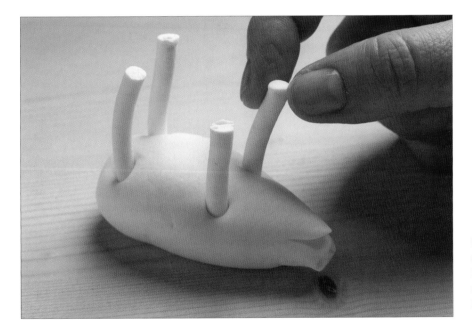

6 Push in two more lengths of candy stick for the front legs. These should be slightly closer together, as the body is narrower here.

7 Make holes for eye sockets with the Dresden tool, then push in glazed black eyes (see page 20). Leave the pig to dry standing up, preferably overnight.

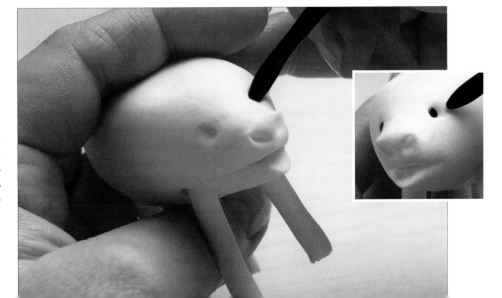

8 Make tiny carrot shapes from Mexican paste and press these on above and below the pig's eyes for eyelids.

9 Make each back leg by rolling a 3.5cm (1³/₈in) cone from 5g (¹/₆oz) of sugarpaste.

10 Flatten the rounded part.

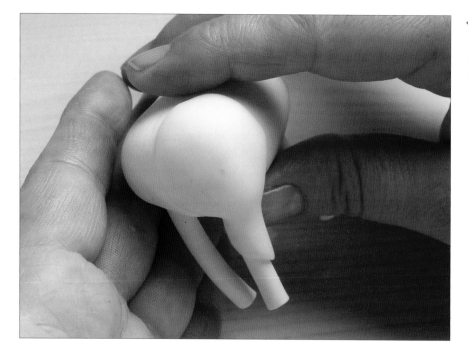

11 Press the sugarpaste leg on to the pig base, moulding it round the candy stick leg and the hip. Repeat for the other back leg.

12 Make the front legs in the same way and press them on, shaping them round the candy stick legs but leaving a bit of bulk for the pig's shoulders.

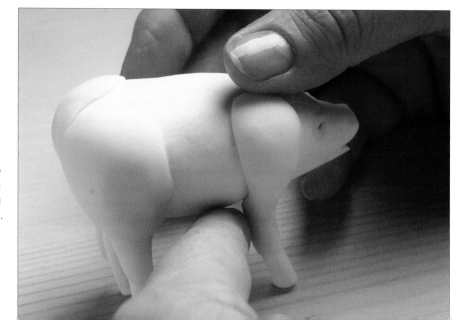

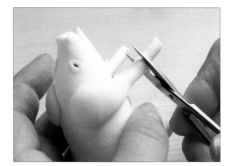

13 Trim the candy sticks to make the legs about 1.5cm (⅝in) long.

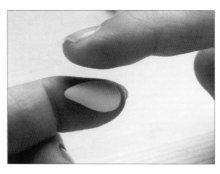

14 Make each ear with a tiny bit of sugarpaste, rolled into a 1.5cm cone.

15 Press each ear with the Dresden tool as shown to hollow them out.

16 Pinch the ends of each ear to shape them. Dampen the ears and press them in place as shown.

17 Dampen the pig's head between the ears. Press sugarpaste through the tea strainer to create fur. Lift it off with the palette knife and place it between the pig's ears.

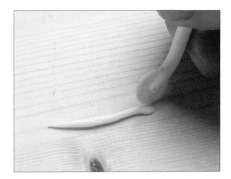

18 Make a 4cm sausage from a tiny bit of sugarpaste. Flatten the end and use the cutting wheel to create fur.

19 Place the tail, pointing upwards.

20 Curl the tail as shown.

The modelled Pig, ready for texturing and colouring.

Above and opposite

The finished Pig. Mark the skin with a palette knife to give texture. Brush all over with a mixture of white and terracotta/skin tone edible powder food colour, brushing slightly more of the terracotta colour on the nose, in the mouth and on the tips of the ears and feet. Brush lightly with dark brown powder colour over the nose and mouth, inside the ears and over the eyes and feet. Finish by adding piping gel to the eyes.

Brown Bear

Brown bears may look cuddly, like the teddy bears we all loved as children, but you would not want to hug a real one of these! They are incredibly powerful, with very sharp claws. Different colours and breeds of bear could be made to suit your requirements.

You will need

86g (just under 3oz) of Mexican paste

2g ($^1/_{12}$oz) of white/champagne sugarpaste

Palette knife

Dresden tool

Ball tool

Tiny amount of black sugarpaste

Edible sugar candy stick

Fine pointed scissors

Fine mesh sieve or tea strainer

Edible powder food colours: dark brown, chocolate brown and black

Confectioner's dusting brush

Kitchen paper

Pure food-grade alcohol

No. 2 paintbrush

Two glazed black eyes (see page 20)

Piping gel in a piping bag

1 Make the body from 40g (1$^1/_3$oz) of Mexican paste. Shape it into an oval and push in a candy stick, right down to the base.

2 Make the arms and legs from 7g (¼oz) of Mexican paste, each shaped into a 4.5cm (1¾in) long carrot.

3 Bend each limb half way down.

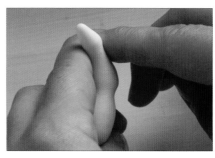

4 Roll each limb between your fingers to create the wrists and ankles.

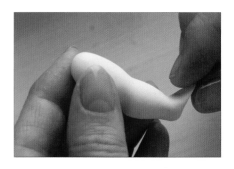

5 Take each of the legs and pinch the end to flatten and widen the foot.

6 Use fine pointed scissors to snip out little triangles to create claws. Make four snips so that there will be five claws.

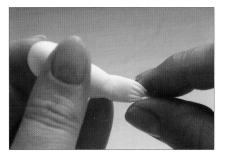

7 Push the claws together by pinching the sides of the foot.

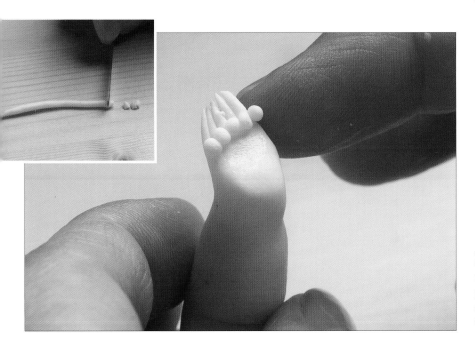

8 To make pads for the back paws, roll a very thin sausage of Mexican paste and cut it into slices: five for each paw. Dampen the underside of each back paw and attach the pads.

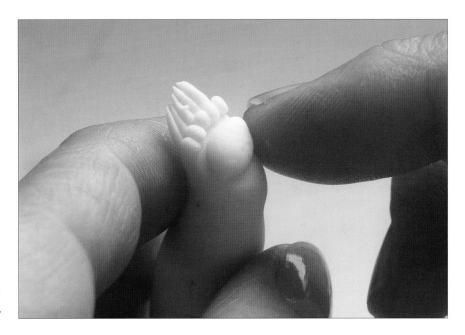

9 Make a tiny ball of Mexican paste for each back paw and press these into place to make the main pads.

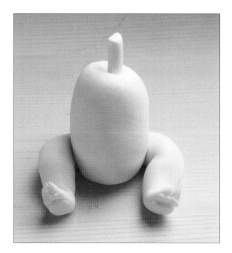

10 Dampen the two back legs and press them into place.

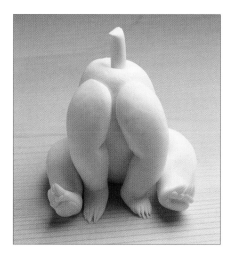

11 The front legs do not need pads on this model as they cannot be seen. Attach them to the body as shown with the flats of the paws on the work surface.

12 Brown bears have a ruff of fur around their neck. To make the fur, push sugarpaste through a tea strainer, lift it off with a palette knife and place it carefully around the dampened neck area.

The Brown Bear with its ruff of fur attached.

13 Take 16g (just over ½oz) of Mexican paste and roll it into a 3.5cm (1³/₈in) pear shape for the head.

14 Mark a line down the centre of the head with the Dresden tool.

15 Make three tiny balls of Mexican paste and place two side by side on the end of the face to make the muzzle, then the third one underneath to make the chin.

16 Press holes in the face to make eye sockets using the Dresden tool.

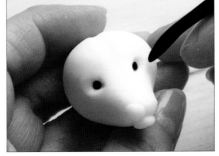

17 Push in two glazed black eyes (see page 20).

18 Make two little carrot shapes from Mexican paste and attach these over the eyes. Blend them in with the Dresden tool.

19 Trim the candy stick neck if necessary. Make a hole in the base of the head using another candy stick, and attach the head to the neck. Make ears from two tiny balls of Mexican paste and attach them to the head.

20 Place a finger behind each ear and use the ball tool to hollow out the ear as shown.

21 Make a tiny ball of black sugarpaste and squeeze it into a triangle for the nose. Push this on to the bear's face.

The modelled Brown Bear, ready for colouring.

Above and opposite

The finished Brown Bear. Brush all over with dark brown edible powder food colour, brushing slightly more firmly on the eyes, the tips of the ears, top to the head and muzzle. Brush gently with black over the pads on the soles of the feet and on the claws on all the feet. Mix a little chocolate brown and dark brown together with pure food-grade alcohol. The mixture needs to be very runny so that the colour runs into the fur on the ruff around the neck. Apply it using the no. 2 paintbrush. Finish by adding piping gel to the eyes.

Kangaroo and Joey

What an amazing design for an animal – having a built-in pouch to carry your baby in! This model has to be perfectly balanced at all stages while it is made, with the candy stick legs ensuring that it stands up well.

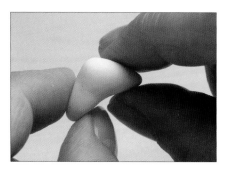

1 Make a double-ended cone from 1.5g ($^{1}/_{16}$oz) of Mexican paste and bend it in the middle to make the Joey's head.

2 Use fine pointed scissors to snip into the head to make the mouth.

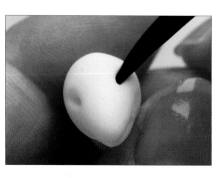

3 Use the Dresden tool to make holes for eye sockets.

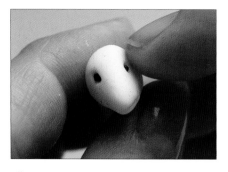

4 Push in chocolate strands for the eyes. Push each strand right in so that only the end shows.

5 To make the ears, shape tiny balls of Mexican paste into cones and squash these with the Dresden tool.

6 Pinch the base of each ear.

You will need

15g (½oz) of Mexican paste

4g ($^{1}/_{6}$oz) of white/champagne sugarpaste

Tiny amount of black sugarpaste

Fine pointed scissors

Dresden tool

Dark chocolate strands

Edible sugar candy sticks

Palette knife

4.5cm (1¾in) oval cutter

Two glazed black eyes (see page 20)

2cm (¾in) circle cutter

Edible powder food colours: autumn gold, terracotta/skin tone and dark brown

Confectioner's dusting brush

Kitchen paper

Piping gel in a piping bag

7 Stick on the ears facing forwards.

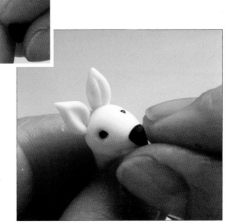

8 Make a tiny ball of black sugarpaste and squeeze it into a triangle for the nose. Dampen and attach to the face.

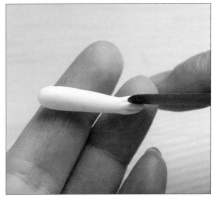

9 Make the main Kangaroo's body from 25g (just under 1oz) of Mexican paste. Shape it into an oval and roll out a long, pointed tail at one end.

10 Push in two 2.5cm (1in) lengths of candy stick for the legs. Make sure the kangaroo balances well between the legs and the tail. Mould the neck and push in a short length of candy stick for the neck. Leave to dry standing up, preferably overnight.

11 Make each foot from 1g (¹/₂₄oz) of Mexican paste rolled into a 2.5cm (1in) carrot. Use the palette knife to mark three toes on each.

12 Blend the feet into the candy stick leg supports.

13 Make each leg with 2g (¹/₁₂oz) of sugarpaste rolled into a 2.5cm (1in) cone.

14 Dampen the legs. Press each leg into the body, being careful not to break the candy sticks. Mould and blend each leg around the candy stick using the Dresden tool.

15 Roll out a small amount of Mexican paste fairly thinly and cut out an oval with a 4.5cm (1¼in) cutter. Cut the oval in half to make the pouch.

16 Lay the Joey's head in the pouch.

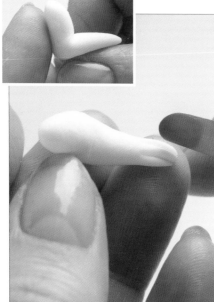

17 Dampen the pouch and press it on to the Kangaroo to attach it.

18 Make each arm by rolling 1g (¹⁄₂₄oz) of Mexican paste into a 3.5cm (1³⁄₈in) carrot shape. Bend each one to make an elbow. Mark the hand with the palette knife to create claws.

19 Dampen the arms and attach them to the Kangaroo.

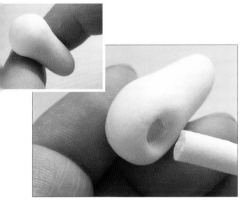
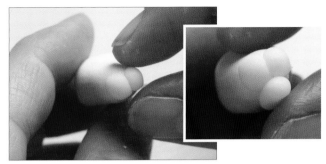

20 Make the main Kangaroo's head with 3g (¹/₈oz) of Mexican paste, rolled into a 2.5cm (1in) pear shape. Make a hole in the base of the head with a candy stick.

21 Roll two tiny balls of Mexican paste and place them on the front of the face to create a snout. Roll a third ball and place it under the first to create the chin.

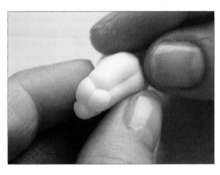
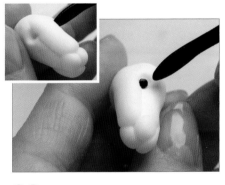
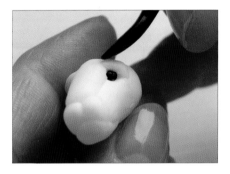

22 Make a carrot shape from 0.5g (¹/₄₈oz) of Mexican paste. Dampen it and stick it to the top of the nose, then blend it in.

23 Use the Dresden tool to make eye sockets and push in glazed black eyes (see page 20).

24 Make tiny carrot shapes from Mexican paste and place them above the eyes to make brows.

25 Take a tiny ball of black sugarpaste, pinch it into a triangle and attach it to make the nose.

26 Trim the candy stick neck if necessary, then dampen and attach the head.

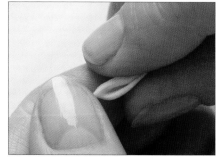

27 Roll out a little Mexican paste thinly, then use a 2cm (¾in) circle cutter to cut out a circle, then an ear shape from the edge of the circle. Make a second ear in the same way.

28 Fold over each ear as shown.

29 Dampen and attach the ears.

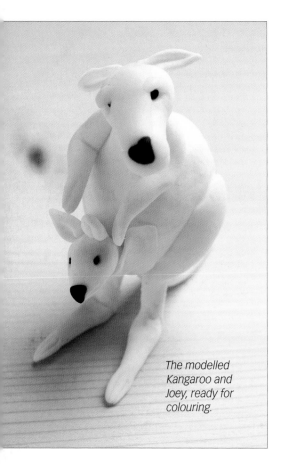

The modelled Kangaroo and Joey, ready for colouring.

Below and opposite

The finished Kangaroo and Joey. Blend together autumn gold and terracotta/skin tone edible powder food colours on kitchen paper. Brush the colour all over. Gently brush dark brown over the feet, the tip of the tail, ears, eyes and mouth. Finish by adding piping gel to the eyes.

Rabbit

My family kept rabbits for a short time when I was a child, but when they started breeding like – well, rabbits, Dad decided it was all getting too much, so it was a rather short-lived hobby.
I decided to make a 'lop-eared' rabbit, just because I like the idea that their ears are so out of proportion with the body. However, you could make your rabbit in different colours and with standard ears if you want to.

You will need

15g (½oz) of Mexican paste
A small amount of white/champagne sugarpaste
Edible sugar candy stick
Dresden tool
Palette knife
Fine mesh sieve or tea strainer
Rolling pin
4.5cm (1¾in) oval cutter
Black edible powder food colour
Pure food-grade alcohol
Two glazed black eyes (see page 20)
Kitchen paper
No. 2 paintbrush
Piping gel and piping bag

1 Make the body from 10g (⅓oz) of Mexican paste rolled into a cone. Push in a 4cm (1½in) length of candy stick for the neck. Mark the shapes of the haunches with the Dresden tool.

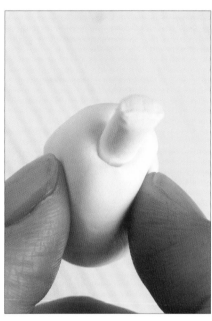

2 Pinch the rabbit's back to shape it.

3 Make each foot from 0.5g (¹⁄₄₈oz) of Mexican paste rolled to a carrot shape. Flatten the end to make the foot and mark the toes with a palette knife.

5 Make the front legs in the same way as the back ones, but bend each one in the middle as shown before marking the toes.

4 Attach the feet under the body as shown.

6 Dampen and attach the front legs as shown.

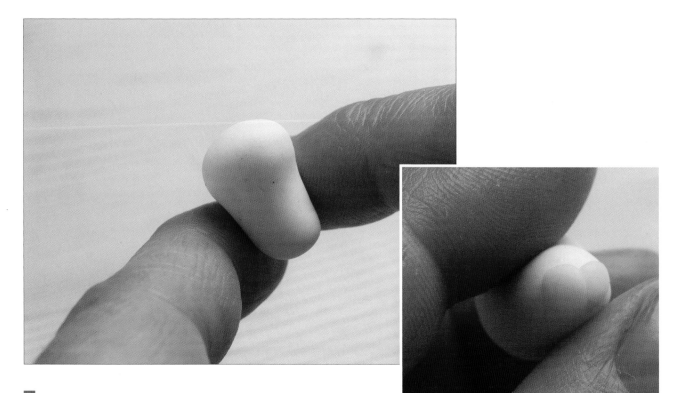

7 Make 2g (¹/₁₂oz) of Mexican paste into a 1.5cm (½in) pear shape for the head. Make two tiny balls of Mexican paste and push them into the narrow end to make the cheeks.

8 Make another tiny ball and press it under the cheeks to make the chin.

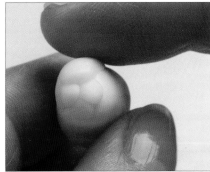

9 Take a tiny piece of Mexican paste and make a cone. Dampen this and press it along the top of the rabbit's face, to make the nose.

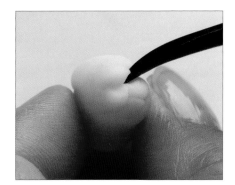

10 Use the Dresden tool to make holes for nostrils.

11 Make holes for eye sockets in the same way.

12 Press in glazed black eyes (see page 20).

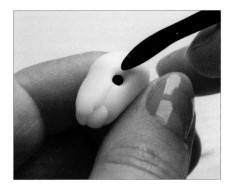

13 Push sugarpaste through the tea strainer to make fur. Pick it up on the palette knife. Dampen the Rabbit's body and use the Dresden tool to help you press on the fur to make a ruff and bib.

14 Press on more fur to make the Rabbit's tail.

15 Roll out a tiny piece of Mexican paste thinly and use a 4.5cm (1¾in) oval cutter to cut out ear shapes as shown.

16 Use the Dresden tool to shape the middle of each ear.

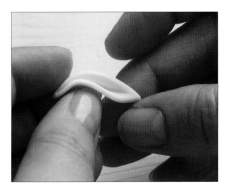

17 Bend each ear as shown to create the lop-eared look for this Rabbit.

18 Dampen and press on the ears as shown.

19 Make more fur in the same way as before and place it on top of the Rabbit's head.

The modelled Rabbit, ready for colouring.

Above and opposite

The finished Rabbit. At this stage the rabbit could be coloured in a number of ways to make different breeds. I chose to make a black and white dappled Rabbit. Mix edible black powder food colour with a few drops of pure food-grade alcohol to make a paint consistency. Paint the ears and feet. To create the dappled effect, the paint on the brush needs to be nearly dry, so dab the brush on to kitchen paper or tissue to separate the hairs. Test the brush on the kitchen paper first to make sure that it is giving a dappled effect, then paint it gently on the Rabbit. Finish by adding piping gel to the eyes.

Rhinoceros

I decided to include the Rhinoceros as another example of an interesting wild and endangered species for people who love wildlife. The hide is made from several different panels, some smooth and some textured.

The patterns for the Rhinoceros.

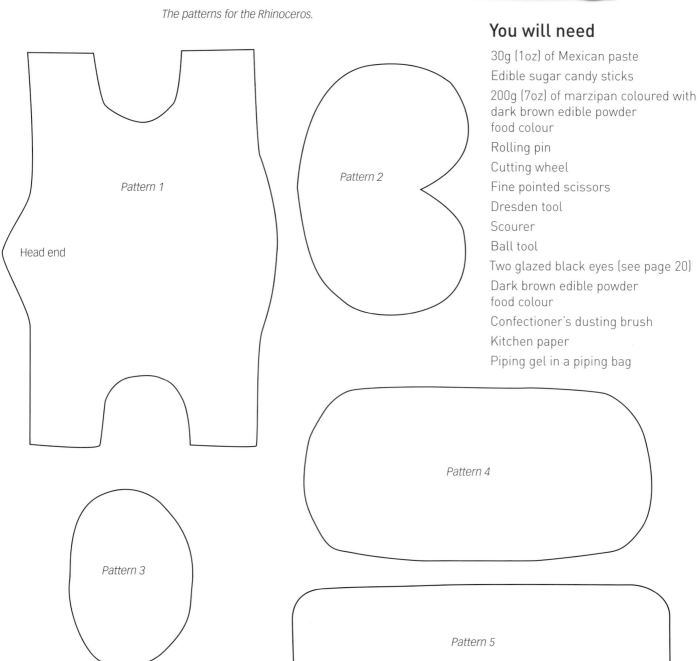

Pattern 1

Head end

Pattern 2

Pattern 3

Pattern 4

Pattern 5

You will need

30g (1oz) of Mexican paste

Edible sugar candy sticks

200g (7oz) of marzipan coloured with dark brown edible powder food colour

Rolling pin

Cutting wheel

Fine pointed scissors

Dresden tool

Scourer

Ball tool

Two glazed black eyes (see page 20)

Dark brown edible powder food colour

Confectioner's dusting brush

Kitchen paper

Piping gel in a piping bag

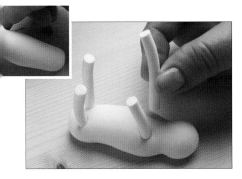

1 Make the body by rolling 30g (1oz) of Mexican or modelling paste into an 8cm (3¹/₈in) sausage, and roll it between your fingers to narrow the neck. Push in four 4.5cm (1¾in) candy sticks for legs as shown and leave to dry, preferably overnight.

2 Roll out coloured marzipan to 2mm (¹/₁₆in) thick. Photocopy or trace pattern 1 and cut it out to make a template. Place this on the marzipan and cut out the shape with a cutting wheel to make the main hide.

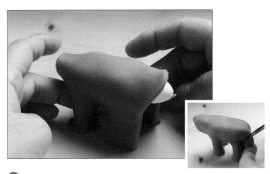

3 Dampen the hide and press it over the body. Trim off any unwanted hide with fine pointed scissors.

4 Press down the fronts of the feet to flatten them a little.

5 Press into the feet with the Dresden tool to make toes.

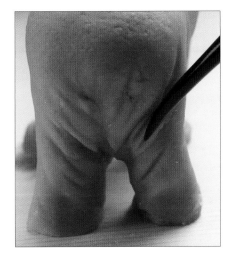

6 Use the Dresden tool to create wrinkles in the hide.

7 Roll out more coloured marzipan, make a template from pattern 2 and cut out the shape to make the rear section of hide. Texture it with the scourer.

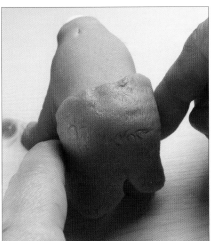

8 Dampen this section of hide and attach it to the rear end of the Rhinoceros.

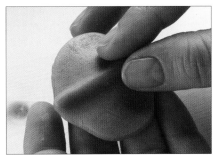

9 Use pattern 3 to make the next section of hide. Pinch a ridge down the centre as shown.

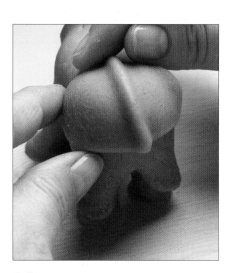

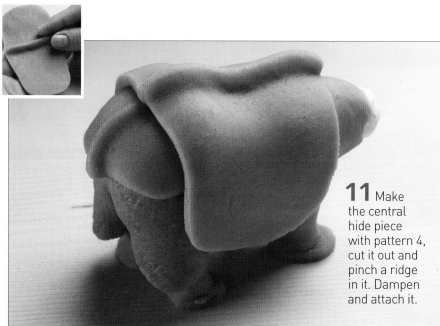

10 Dampen the piece of hide and attach it over the rear section as shown.

11 Make the central hide piece with pattern 4, cut it out and pinch a ridge in it. Dampen and attach it.

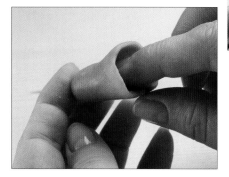

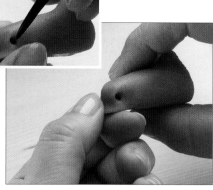

12 Make the head from 10g (¹/₃oz) of the coloured marzipan rolled into a 3cm (1¹/₈in) sausage. Hollow it out with a ball tool and then widen it with your fingers and lengthen it to 4cm (1½in) long.

13 Flatten the bottom of the head a little and make holes for nostrils with the Dresden tool. Pinch out the mouth to create a lip shape.

14 Push up the lip to create the distinctive mouth shape of the Rhinoceros.

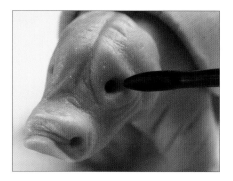

15 Push the head on to the body and blend it in.

16 Add wrinkles and eye sockets using the Dresden tool.

17 Push in two glazed black eyes (see page 20).

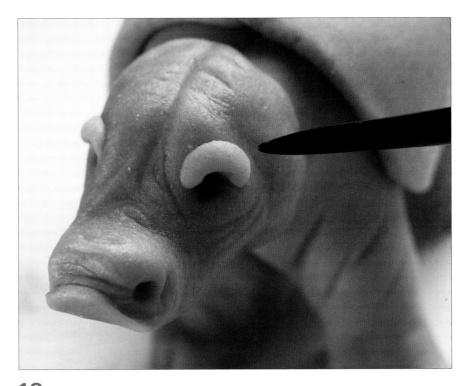

18 Make brows from small carrot shapes of coloured marzipan and stick these over the eyes. Blend the eyebrows in and make them look more wrinkly with the Dresden tool.

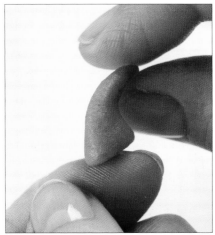

19 Make the Rhinoceros's all-important horn using 1g of coloured marzipan, formed into a cone and curved as shown.

20 Dampen and attach the horn, then blend it in with the Dresden tool.

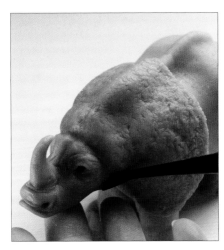

21 Make the final section of hide using pattern 5, and texture it with the scourer. Dampen it, press it in place and blend it in.

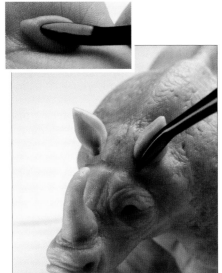

22 Make each ear from 0.5g (¹/₄₈oz) of coloured marzipan shaped into a carrot. Press with the Dresden tool to hollow each one out. Dampen and attach the ears.

*The modelled Rhinoceros,
ready for colouring.*

Left and opposite

*The finished Rhinoceros. Brush dark brown
edible powder food colour over the edges
of the layers of hide, the toes, the ridge
down the back, and round the eyes, mouth,
nostrils, the tip of the ears and the horn.
Finish by adding piping gel to
the eyes.*

Baby Elephant

Years ago I watched a documentary series which followed a herd of elephants over a few months. I was struck by the strength of the family bond, and how the aunts were such an important help in the care of the baby elephants. This baby elephant was lovely to make. Using marzipan for the skin means that you can easily blend in extra marzipan to fill any areas which may look too thin, even when the model has had time to dry. This also means that you could make this into an older, fatter elephant by adding extra marzipan for the tummy. It would be a good idea to let the first layer of skin on the model dry before adding the extra weight. You could also then make a pair of tusks from Mexican paste to insert into the sides of the trunk.

You will need

30g (1oz) of Mexican or modelling paste

Edible sugar candy sticks

150g (5¼oz) marzipan coloured with dark brown edible food colour powder

Rolling pin

Cutting wheel

Dresden tool

Semicircle tool

Palette knife

Fine pointed scissors

Two glazed black eyes (see page 20)

Dark brown edible powder food colour

Confectioner's dusting brush

Kitchen paper

Piping gel in a piping bag

The patterns for the Baby Elephant.

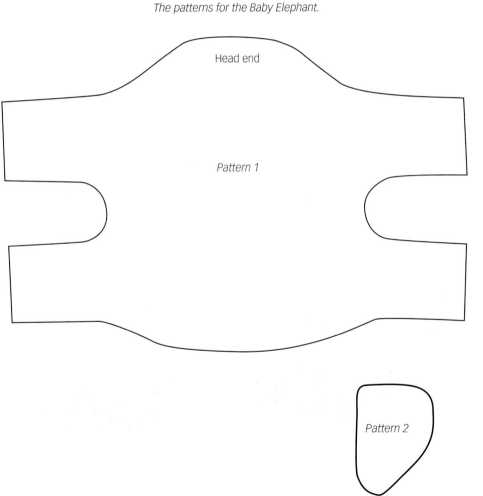

Head end

Pattern 1

Pattern 2

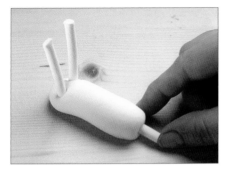

1 Make the body from 30g (1oz) of Mexican or modelling paste rolled into a 7cm (2¾in) sausage shape. Put in four 6cm (2³⁄₈in) candy stick legs and a short length of candy stick for the neck.

2 Stand the elephant base up and leave it to dry, preferably overnight.

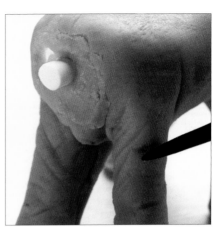

3 Photocopy or trace pattern 1 for the elephant hide and cut it out to make a template. Roll out coloured marzipan to 3mm (¹⁄₈in) thick and cut round the template using a cutting wheel. Press the hide on to the body and use the Dresden tool to create wrinkles.

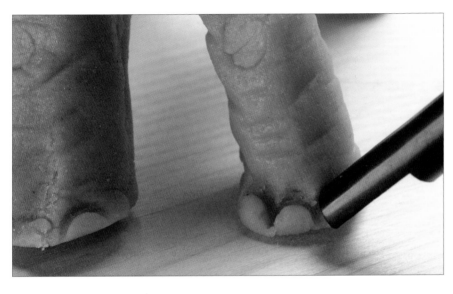

4 Use the semicircle tool to create the Elephant's toes.

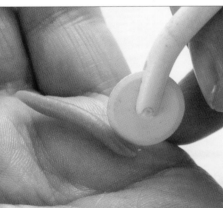

5 Make the tail by rolling a tiny amount of coloured marzipan. Flatten the end and use the cutting wheel to create hairs.

6 Dampen and attach the tail.

7 Make a template from pattern 2 and use this to cut out two ear shapes from rolled out coloured marzipan. Use the Dresden tool to press indentations very close to each other on the outer edge of the ears; this will give a ridged and frilled effect.

8 Fold over the tops of the ears as shown.

9 Make the head from 15g (½oz) of coloured marzipan and roll it out to form a trunk. The total length should be 7cm (2¾in).

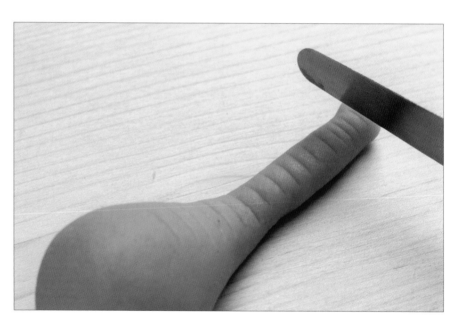

10 Use the palette knife to mark wrinkles on the trunk.

11 Mark nostrils in the end of the trunk using the Dresden tool.

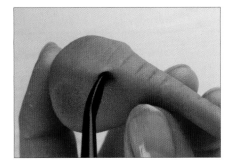

12 Mark eye sockets with the Dresden tool.

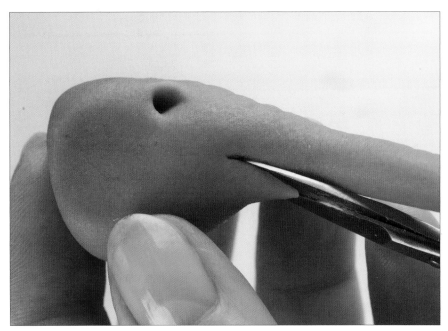

13 Snip a mouth under the trunk with fine pointed scissors.

14 Press two glazed black eyes (see page 20) into the eye sockets. Attach the head to the body and blend it in with the Dresden tool.

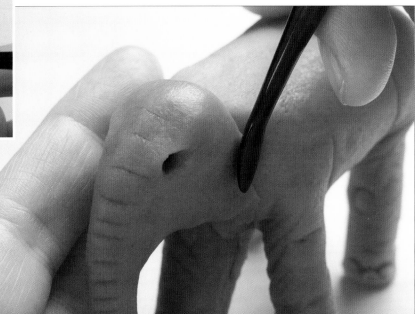

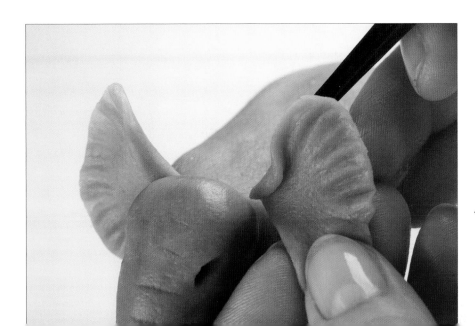

15 Dampen and attach the ears.

The modelled Baby Elephant, ready for colouring.

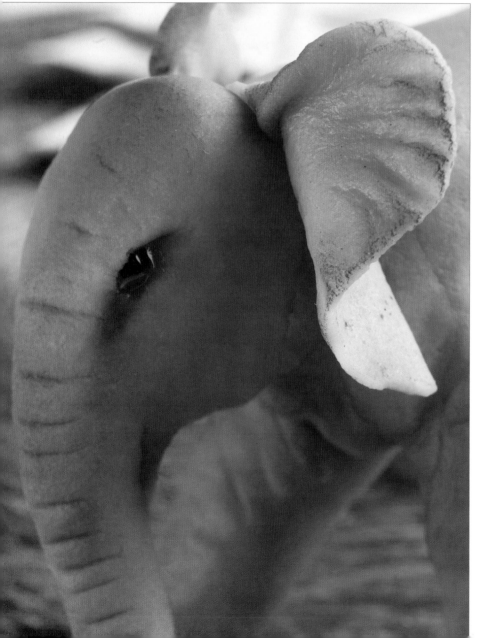

Left and opposite

The finished Baby Elephant. Gently brush with dark brown edible powder food colour over the edges of the ears, eyes, the top of the head, trunk, mouth, toes and wrinkles. The dusting is intended to highlight the features rather than colour them. Finish by adding piping gel to the eyes.

Tortoise

Lots of people had tortoises when I was a child, including our next-door neighbour. I used to sit and watch this tortoise, fascinated by how it ate cabbage and lettuce leaves. Tortoises were so popular as pets that every year on 'Blue Peter', a British children's programme, they explained how to get the tortoise ready for hibernation in the winter. In making this tortoise model I have made it paler than real life, so that the patterns in the shell can be seen.

You will need

100g (3½oz) of marzipan
Fine pointed scissors
Dresden tool
No. 2 piping nozzle
Palette knife
Edible powder food colours: dark brown and dark foliage green
Rolling pin
6cm (2⅜in) circle cutter
Fine palette knife
Confectioner's dusting brush
Kitchen paper
Two glazed black eyes (see page 20)

1 Make the body from 15g (½oz) of marzipan rolled into a 4cm (1½in) oval.

2 Make the head from 3g (⅛oz) of marzipan shaped into a cone.

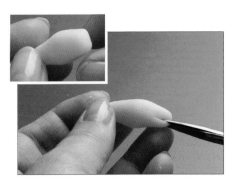

3 Square off the front of the head and snip the mouth with fine pointed scissors.

4 Mark nostrils with the Dresden tool.

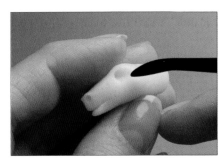

5 Make holes for the eye sockets in the same way.

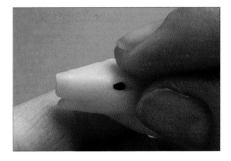

6 Push in glazed black eyes (see page 20) and pinch the sockets to close them a little.

7 Make each of the two front legs by rolling 2g (¹/₁₂oz) of marzipan into a 3cm (1¹/₈in) carrot. Curve each leg a little.

8 Mark each leg all over with the no. 2 piping nozzle to create the reptilian texture.

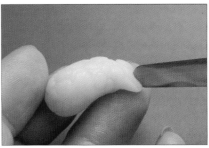

10 Make two back legs in the same way, but make them shorter and fatter than the front legs. Mark the toes in the same way.

9 Use the palette knife to mark each foot to create toes.

11 Roll a tiny tail from marzipan. Dampen all the pieces and attach them to the body.

12 Brush dark foliage green edible powder food colour over the head, legs and tail and the lower half of the body near the works surface, just in case the shell doesn't cover it. There is no need to colour the top of the body as it will be hidden under the shell.

13 Now make the Tortoise's shell. Mix dark foliage green edible powder food colour in with 30g (1oz) of plain marzipan but leave it only partially mixed to create a marbled effect. Roll out a 10 x 6cm (4 x 2³/₈in) rectangle of the marbled marzipan.

14 Brush all over the surface of the rectangle with dark brown edible powder food colour using a confectioner's dusting brush.

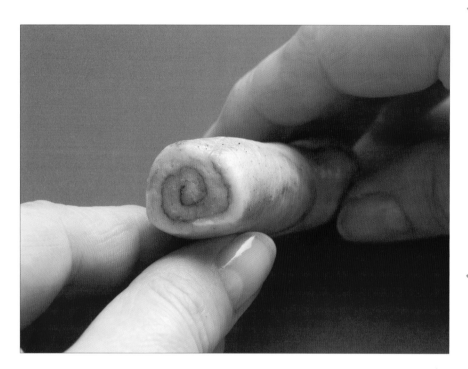

15 Roll up the rectangle to create a marbled spiral effect. Wrap the rolled-up marzipan in plastic food wrap and leave it for at least one hour for the spiral to stick together.

16 Cut the roll into even slices using the fine palette knife.

17 Thoroughly mix dark foliage green edible powder food colour with 30g (1oz) of marzipan and roll it out 2mm (¹⁄₁₆in) thick. Cut out a 6cm (2¼in) diameter circle. Lay the slices on the circle. Cut half circles to place round the edge.

18 Roll gently with a rolling pin.

19 Push and smooth the edges to return it to its circular shape.

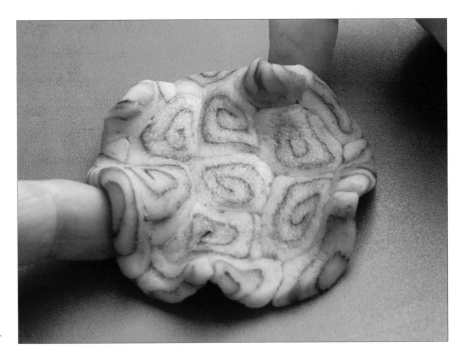

20 Place a finger under the shell to make a curve for the head, and repeat for each of the legs.

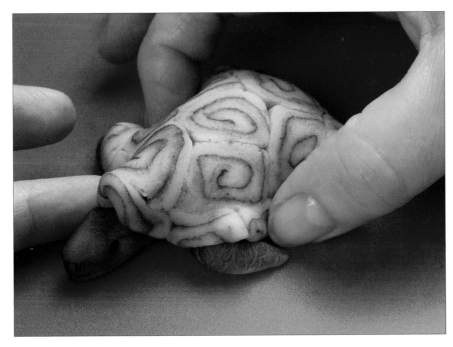

21 Dampen the underside of the shell and press it on to the Tortoise.

Polar Bear

Using natural rather than coloured marzipan for the Polar Bear gives a very realistic colour, as well as the lovely properties of modelling with marzipan. Polar bears are another memory from childhood – I saw an unhappy looking one in a zoo in a dark grey concrete pen which I suppose was meant to look like ice!

The pattern for the Polar Bear's fur.

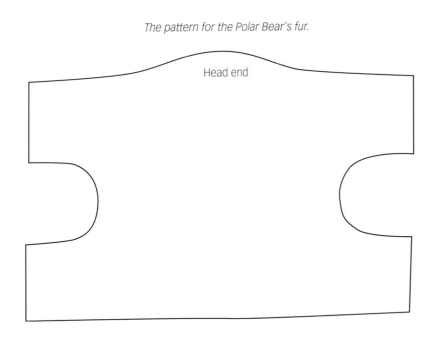

Head end

You will need

25g (just under 1oz) of Mexican paste

Edible sugar candy sticks

115g (4oz) of marzipan

Tiny amount of black sugarpaste

Cutting wheel

Scourer

Dresden tool

Fine pointed scissors

Dark brown edible powder food colour

Confectioner's dusting brush

Kitchen paper

Two glazed black eyes (see page 20)

Piping gel in a piping bag

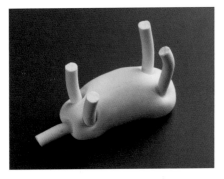

1 Make the body from 25g (just under 1oz) of Mexican paste rolled into a sausage shape. Push in two 4.5cm (1¾in) lengths of candy stick for the back legs and two 3.5 lengths (1³⁄₈in) for the front legs. Stand the body upright and leave it to dry, preferably overnight.

2 Roll out 100g (3½oz) of marzipan 3mm (¹⁄₈in) thick. Photocopy or trace the pattern and cut it out to make a template. Lay it on the marzipan and cut out the shape with a cutting wheel. Texture the marzipan with the scourer to create the Polar Bear's fur.

3 Dampen the underside of the fur, lay it over the body and press it around the legs.

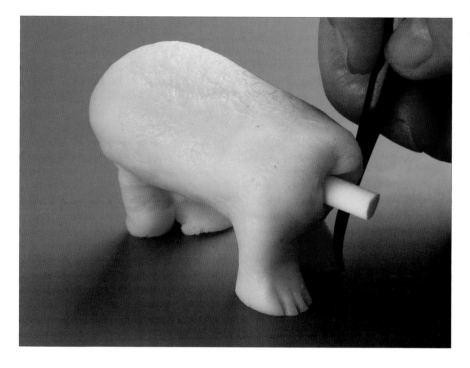

4 Shape the fur over the body. Push out the marzipan over the fronts of the feet and mark claws with the Dresden tool.

5 Make the head from 10g (1/3oz) of marzipan rolled into a pear shape 3cm (1 1/8in) long.

6 Square off the muzzle by pressing with your thumb.

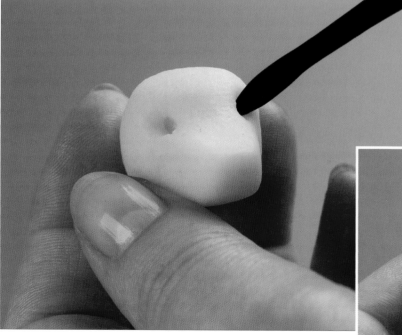

7 Use the Dresden tool to make eye sockets and press in glazed black eyes (see page 20).

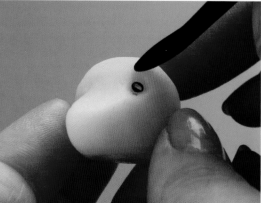

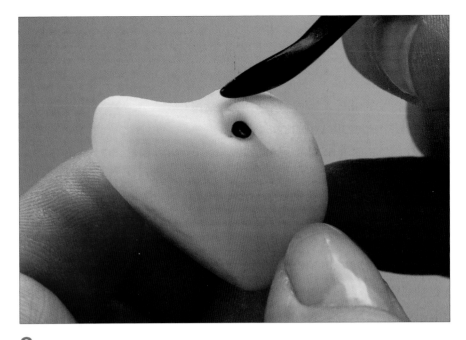

9 Take a tiny ball of black sugarpaste and pinch it into a triangle for the nose.

8 Roll two tiny carrot shapes from marzipan and press them over the eyes to make brows. Blend them in with the Dresden tool.

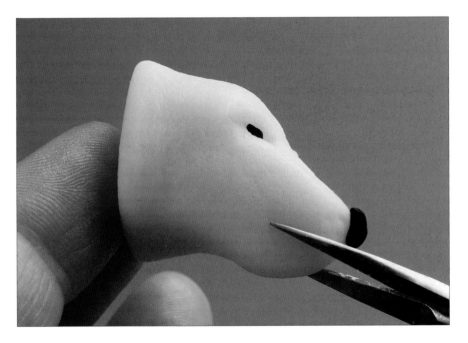

10 Dampen and attach the nose and use fine pointed scissors to snip a mouth underneath.

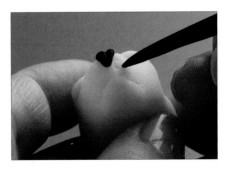

11 Use the Dresden tool to mark dots around the nose for whiskers.

12 Use your finger and thumb to hollow out the back of the head ready to attach it to the body.

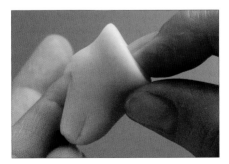

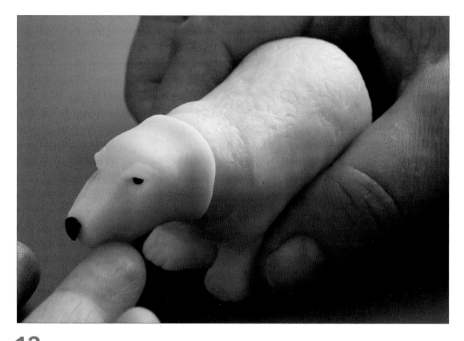

13 Trim the candy stick neck to size if necessary, then push on the head.

14 Make a sausage of marzipan and roll it flat, then place it over the join where the head meets the body.

15 Drag the added marzipan with the Dresden tool to blend it in and to add texture.

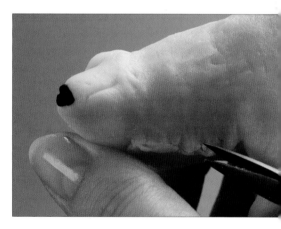

16 Snip around the bottom of the neck with fine pointed scissors to create the texture of long fur.

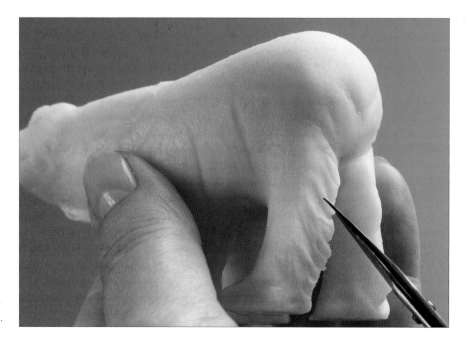

17 Snip the backs of the legs to create the look of long fur here.

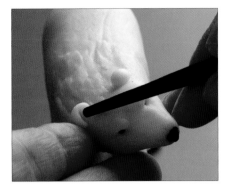

18 Make two tiny balls of marzipan for ears. Dampen them and attach them in place. Support each ear with a finger while you hollow out the inside with a tool.

The modelled Polar Bear ready for colouring.

Left and opposite

The finished Polar Bear. Brush dark brown edible powder food colour gently on the feet, tail, eyebrows, mouth, the front of the face, inside the ears and on the ends of the snipped fur. Paint a little piping gel on the nose and in each eye.

Three Cats

These are my own cats. They have been with us since 2004. I have made them using plain sugarpaste without adding any gum as they are relatively simple shapes and do not need the extra strength to hold them up. You may prefer to use a modelling paste that you are used to.

Asher

Asher came to us as a rescue cat, as she had been living on the street. She has two very distinct characters – in the bedroom she loves being stroked and fussed, out of the bedroom no one can approach her, as she thinks she is going to be attacked!

You will need

45g (1½oz) of white/champagne sugarpaste

Small amount of green sugarpaste

Edible sugar candy stick

Dresden tool

Palette knife

Fine pointed scissors

Edible powder food colours: white and black

Confectioner's dusting brush

Kitchen paper

Pure food-grade alcohol

Piping gel in a piping bag

Fine paintbrush

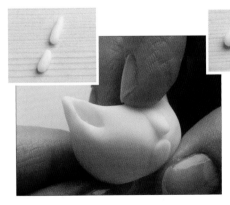

1 Make a 3cm (1⅛in) oval shape from 10g (⅓oz) of sugarpaste and gently pinch two ears.

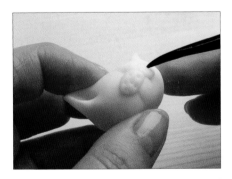

2 Use the Dresden tool to hollow out the ears.

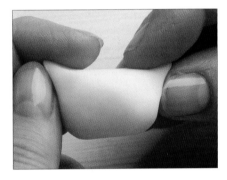

3 Make a tiny cone shape for the nose and a tiny oval shape for the chin and press them in place.

4 Make two tiny ovals for cheeks, and press them on to the cat.

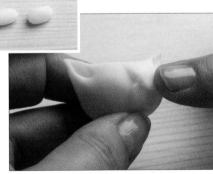

5 Mark dots for whiskers with the pointed end of the Dresden tool.

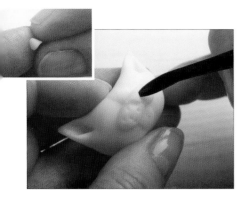

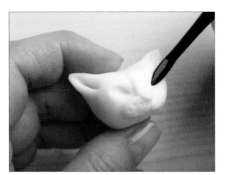

6 Take a tiny ball of sugarpaste and pinch it into a triangle for the nose. Press the nose on gently, then push upwards on either side with the Dresden tool to make nostrils.

7 Push in the Dresden tool on either side of the nose to make eye sockets.

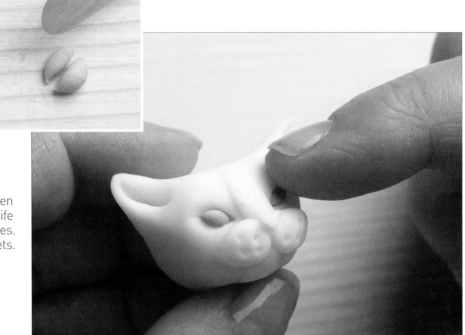

8 Make a tiny oval of green sugarpaste and use the palette knife to cut it in half to make the eyes. Press these into the eye sockets.

9 For the body, take 30g (1oz) of sugarpaste and roll and shape it in your hands to make a 6cm (2³⁄₈in) long cone.

10 Cut through the pointed end with a palette knife to separate the two front legs.

11 Twist each leg so that the cut edge is against your work surface.

12 Use the knife to make little marks in the ends of the paws to suggest claws.

13 Press your finger where the head will go to make an indentation.

14 Push in a 3cm (1⅛in) length of candy stick for the neck.

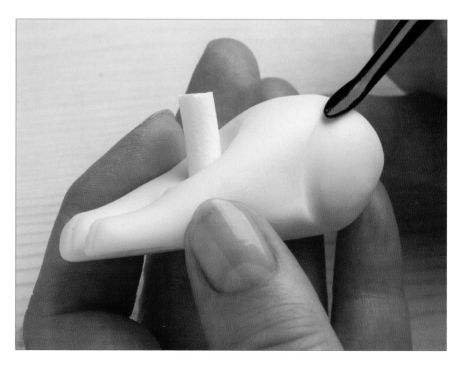

15 Mark the cat's haunches on both sides with the Dresden tool.

16 For the tail, roll out 3g (¹/₈oz) of sugarpaste into a 6cm (2³/₈in) long sausage.

17 Stick the tail on to the cat with a little water.

18 Trim the candy stick neck with scissors if necessary. Push a length of candy stick into the head to make a hole, and place the head on the neck.

The modelled cat, ready for colouring.

The finished cat. Blend black and white edible powder food colour to get a nice grey. Brush all over the cat. Mix black powder with pure food-grade alcohol and paint a large black circle in the middle of each eye with a fine paintbrush. When the paint is dry, add piping gel to the surface of the eyes.

Colleen

Colleen is by far the laziest and fattest of our three cats, so I had to make her asleep! When we moved to our cottage, she scared herself, and us, by getting stuck up a tree twice. We had to help her down when we finally found her.

You will need

45g (1½oz) of white sugarpaste

Edible sugar candy stick

Dresden tool

Palette knife

Fine pointed scissors

Edible powder food colours: autumn gold, dark brown, black and soft pink

Pure food-grade alcohol

No. 2 paintbrush and kitchen paper

1 Follow steps 1 to 6 as for Asher, then use a palette knife to mark closed eyes.

2 Take 30g (1oz) of sugarpaste and roll it to make the body, then roll out the tail from one end to make a total length of 10cm (4in).

3 Curve the tail round the body.

4 Use the Dresden tool to mark the haunch for the back leg. Mark one side only for this cat.

5 Make an indent with your finger for the head, then put in a 3cm (1⅛in) length of candy stick.

6 Trim the stick if necessary with scissors. Make an indent in the head with a piece of candy stick, then push it on the neck.

The modelled cat and the finished version. Using the no. 2 paintbrush, gently brush pale soft pink powder on the nose. ery gently brush dark brown powder colour in the closed eyes and the mouth. Mix the autumn gold with pure food-grade alcohol to make a paint consistency. Paint the gold markings. Mix the black powder in the same way and paint the black markings.

Riamh

The name is pronounced 'Reeve'. This lovely-natured cat has a habit of rolling over on her back to show off her white tummy whenever she can, so this is how I have modelled her.

You will need

45g (1½oz) of white/champagne sugarpaste

Small amount of green sugarpaste

Edible sugar candy stick

Dresden tool

Palette knife

Fine pointed scissors

No. 16 piping nozzle

No. 2 piping nozzle

Edible powder food colours: dark brown and black

Confectioner's dusting brush

Kitchen paper

Pure food-grade alcohol

No. 2 paintbrush

Piping gel in a piping bag

1 Make the head as for Asher, steps 1 to 8. Take 30g (1oz) of sugarpaste and roll out a body and tail to a length of 10cm (4in).

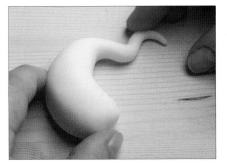

2 Curve the body and tail as shown.

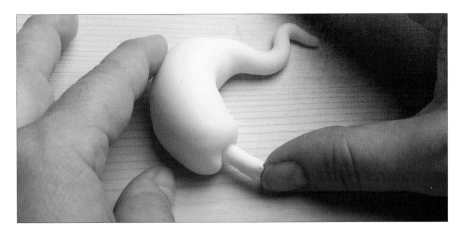

3 Push in a 3cm (1⅛in) length of candy stick for the neck.

4 Roll out four carrot shapes for paws, each from 1g (¹/₂₄oz) of sugarpaste.

5 Mark all four paws with the knife to make claws.

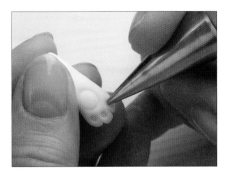

6 Take the two back paws and mark the footpad with the no. 16 piping nozzle and the toe pads with the no. 2 piping nozzle.

7 Stick on the back paws with a little water. Stick on the front paws in the same way.

8 Fold down the front paws as shown.

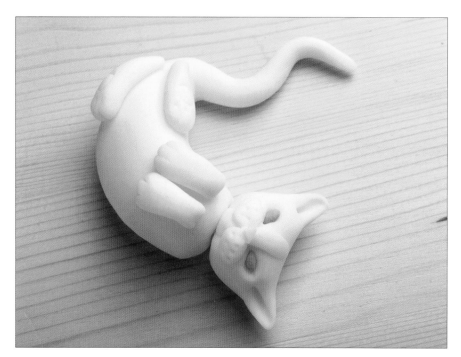

The modelled cat, ready for colouring. At the final stage, the neck has been trimmed with scissors and an indent made in the head with a candy stick. The head has then been attached.

The finished cat. Use a confectioner's dusting brush with dark brown powder food colour to colour the tail, legs, back and sides of the body and the head, leaving the cheeks and tummy white. Mix a little dark brown powder with pure food-grade alcohol to a paint consistency. Paint the nose and outline the eyes, then paint the tips of the ears, wiggly stripes across the tail and legs, stripes on the side of the body and stripes on the head. Paint a large black circle in the middle of each eye with a fine paintbrush. When it is dry, add piping gel to the surface of each eye.

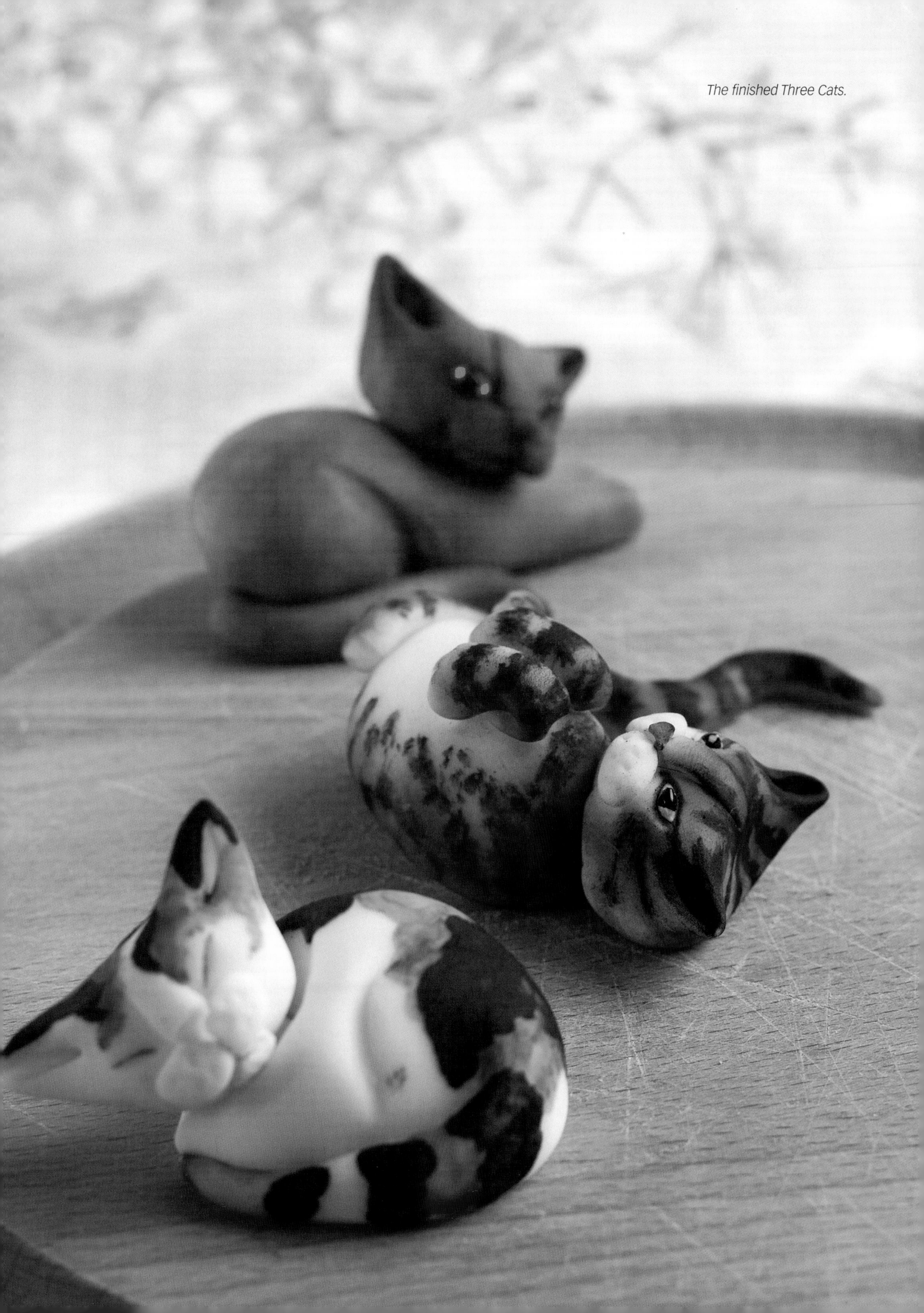

The finished Three Cats.

Bat

We have bats in the roof of our cottage, and at dusk we can see them coming out from under the eaves. They flit around in different directions, catching insects. They are too fast to have a proper look, so I had to rely on the internet for the detail. This is the only model in the book which contains non-edible items. If you make this Bat for a cake, you must let people know that the wings cannot be eaten due to the inclusion of wires for support.

You will need

10g (¹⁄₃oz) of sugarpaste
100g (3½oz) of Mexican paste or flower paste
Cocktail stick
Brushpen
Fine mesh sieve or tea strainer
Palette knife
Dresden tool
Dark chocolate strands
Eight 12cm (4¾in) 33g fine florist's wires
Florist's tape
Rolling pin
Cutting wheel
Fine pointed scissors
Dark brown edible powder food colour
Pure food-grade alcohol
No. 2 paintbrush
Confectioner's dusting brush
Kitchen paper

1 Make an oval-shaped body from 5g (¹⁄₆oz) of sugarpaste and put in a cocktail stick for ease of handling

2 Dampen the oval using a brushpen, leaving the back dry.

3 Push sugarpaste through a fine mesh sieve or tea strainer as shown here, to create fur.

4 Use a palette knife to lift the fur-textured sugarpaste from the tea strainer.

5 Apply the fur to the dampened sugarpaste body.

6 Add more fur as required. Make an indent for the head with your finger.

7 Make holes for the legs using the Dresden tool.

8 Make a little leg 1.5cm (⅝in) long and use the palette knife to make two marks for toes.

9 Curl the end of the toes over as shown. Make a second leg in the same way.

10 Dampen the ends of the legs and stick them in the holes.

11 Shape a pea-sized piece of sugarpaste to a cone and use the Dresden tool to mark two nostrils.

12 Press in two chocolate strands for eyes.

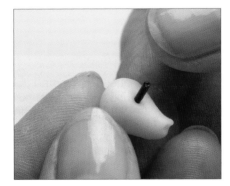

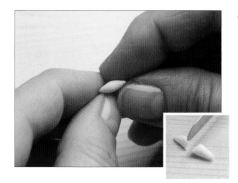

13 For the ears, make a tiny sausage shape from sugarpaste and squeeze it to a point at both ends. Cut it in half.

14 Hollow out each ear with the Dresden tool.

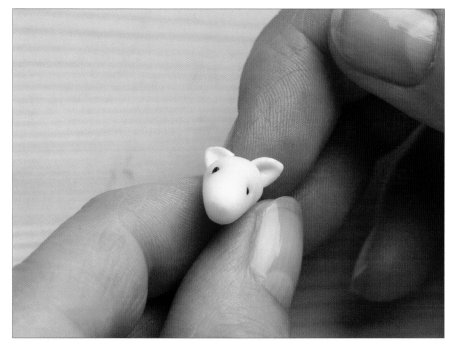

15 Dampen the head and stick on the ears.

16 Stick the head into the indent on the body.

17 Tape four florist's wires together with florist's tape half-way down.

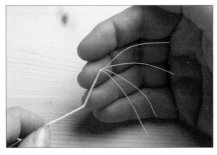

18 Bend and curve the wires into a wing shape as shown. Make a second wing in the same way.

19 Thinly roll out enough Mexican or flower paste to cover the wing.

20 Wrap a pea-sized piece of the Mexican or flower paste around the base of a spoke.

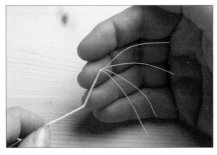

21 Use your finger and thumb to 'wiggle' the Mexican or flower paste around the spoke. It rolls around the wire and coats it to the end. Repeat for each spoke. Pinch off the excess paste at the ends.

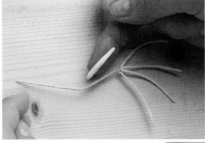

22 Dampen the main wire of the wing and attach a sausage of Mexican or flower paste to it. Repeat steps 20–22 for the other wing.

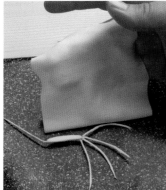

23 Dampen the paste-covered wires with a little water. Lift up the rolled out Mexican or flower paste, place it over a wing and press it with your fingers.

24 Cut round the edges of the wires with a cutting wheel. Cut curves between the spokes in the style of a bat's wing.

The finished wing. Complete the second wing in the same way.

25 Curve the wires to shape the wings and trim the base wires to 1cm (³/₈in) with scissors.

26 Push the wings into the back of the body and pull out the cocktail stick.

The modelled Bat, ready for colouring.

Left and opposite

The finished Bat. Brush dark brown edible powder food colour very gently over the wings to keep them pale. Brush more over the ears, feet and face, and make it slightly darker over the nose. Mix a little dark brown together with pure food-grade alcohol. Apply the paint to the fur with the no. 2 paintbrush. The mixture needs to be very runny so that the colour runs right into the fur (see page 19).

Index

bat 7, 11, 120–127
  wing 124, 125, 126
beaver 9, 40–45
blend 25, 31, 37, 41, 48, 60, 61, 73, 77, 78, 79, 80, 90, 91, 97, 109
brown bear 70–75
brows 31, 37, 40, 44, 48, 53, 56, 61, 79, 91, 108, 110
brushpen 10, 11, 19, 20, 126

CMC (cellulose gum) 8, 21
cake decorating 6, 46
cat 7, 12, 19, 21, 112–119
chocolate strands 9, 23, 76, 120, 122
claws 70, 71, 74, 78, 107, 114, 117
colouring 6, 10, 11, 18, 26, 32, 44, 50, 55, 62, 68, 74, 86, 92, 98, 110, 115, 118, 126
confectioner's dusting brush 11, 18, 22, 26, 28, 32, 38, 40, 46, 52, 58, 62, 64, 70, 76, 88, 94, 100, 102, 106, 112, 117, 118, 120
cow 28–33

Dresden tool 10, 14, 21, 22, 24, 25, 28, 31, 34, 35, 37, 38, 40, 41, 42, 43, 46, 47, 53, 54, 58, 61, 64, 65, 67, 73, 76, 78, 79, 82, 84, 85, 88, 89, 90, 94, 96, 97, 100, 106, 107, 108, 109, 112, 113, 114, 116, 117, 120, 121, 122, 123

ear 24, 25, 26, 31, 32, 38, 41, 44, 46, 50, 54, 62, 67, 68, 73, 74, 76, 77, 80, 85, 86, 91, 92, 95, 96, 98, 110, 112, 118, 123, 126
edible powder food colour 11, 16, 18, 19, 20, 21, 22, 26, 28, 32, 34, 38, 40, 44, 46, 50, 52, 56, 58, 62, 68, 70, 74, 76, 80, 82, 86, 88, 92, 94, 100, 101, 102, 103, 106, 110, 112 115, 116, 117, 118, 120, 126
edible sugar candy sticks 9, 21, 2 28, 34, 58, 64, 70, 82, 88, 94, 106 112, 116, 117
elephant 94–99
  hide 95
  trunk 96, 97, 98
eye(s) 9, 11, 20, 21, 23, 32, 38, 44 46, 48, 50, 53, 56, 58, 62, 66, 68, 76, 80, 86, 91, 92, 98, 110, 116, 1

glazed black 11, 20, 31, 34, 37, 40, 41, 46, 47, 52, 53, 58, 61, 65, 70, 73, 76, 79, 82, 84, 88, 90, 94, 97, 100, 106, 107
eye socket 10, 21, 30, 37, 41, 47, 48, 53, 61, 65, 73, 76, 79, 84, 90, 97, 100, 107, 113

flower paste 8, 120, 124, 125
fox 7, 52–57
fur 8, 10, 12, 15, 16, 17, 19, 38, 44, 54, 55, 56, 58, 60, 62, 67, 68, 72, 74, 84, 85, 106, 107, 109, 110, 120, 121, 126

gorilla 9, 11, 12, 16, 17, 34–39

joey 76–81

kangaroo 76–81
  pouch 78

lion 58–63
  mane 61, 62

marzipan 8, 9, 11, 12, 15, 88, 89, 90, 91, 94, 95, 96, 100, 101, 102, 103, 106, 107, 108, 109, 110
meerkat 46–51
Mexican paste 8, 9, 12, 20, 21, 22, 28, 32, 34, 36, 40, 46, 48, 49, 50, 52, 55, 58, 60, 64, 66, 70, 71, 73, 76, 77, 78, 79, 80, 82, 83, 84, 85, 88, 89, 94, 95, 106, 120, 124, 125
modelling 6, 8, 10, 20, 21, 32
modelling paste 8, 28, 34, 36, 46, 48, 49, 58, 60, 89, 94, 95, 112
muzzle 30, 31, 36, 37, 40, 42, 73, 74, 107

painting 19, 32
pig 7, 64–69
piping bag 11, 16, 20, 21, 28, 34, 40, 46, 52, 58, 64, 70, 76, 88, 94, 106, 112

piping gel 9, 20, 21, 28, 32, 34, 38, 40, 44, 46, 50, 52, 56, 58, 62, 64, 68, 70, 74, 76, 80, 86, 88, 92, 94, 98, 106, 110, 112, 115, 118
polar bear 14, 18, 20, 106–111
pure food-grade alcohol 11, 19, 22, 32, 34, 38, 52, 56, 58, 62, 70, 74, 82, 86, 112, 115, 116, 117, 120, 126
rabbit 82–87
rhinoceros 88–93
  hide 88, 89, 90, 91, 92
  horn 91, 92
royal icing 9, 10, 11, 16, 17, 34, 38

scourer 10, 14, 22, 25, 88, 89, 91, 106
sculpting 8, 10
sheep 7, 22–27, 28, 31, 54
sugarcraft 6, 9, 16
sugarpaste 8, 9, 12, 15, 18, 21, 22, 23, 24, 25, 28, 29, 30, 31, 34, 36, 37, 38, 40, 41, 42, 43, 44, 48, 52, 53, 54, 55, 58, 60, 61, 62, 64, 66, 67, 68, 70, 72, 74, 76, 77, 82, 84, 106, 108, 112, 113, 115, 116, 117, 120, 121, 122, 123

tail 32, 40, 43, 44, 50, 55, 60, 62, 68, 77, 80, 95, 101, 115, 116, 117, 118
tea strainer 10, 15, 28, 31, 52, 54, 55, 58, 61, 67, 70, 72, 82, 84, 120, 121
teeth 40, 42, 44
texture(d) 8, 10, 14, 16, 17, 19, 23, 25, 38, 44, 68, 88, 89, 91, 101, 106, 109, 121
tortoise 100–105
  shell 100, 101, 102, 103

whiskers 42, 61, 108, 112
wrinkles 37, 89, 90, 95, 96, 98